OREGON
HUNTING GUIDE

By John A. Johnson

OREGON
HUNTING GUIDE

Copyright 1988 by John Johnson

ISBN 0912299-39-8 (Hardcover)
ISBN 0912299-40-1 (Softcover)

Cover Photo: This collection of photographs has been provided by the Oregon Department of Fish and Game.

STONEYDALE PRESS PUBLISHING COMPANY
205 Main Street — Drawer B
Stevensville, Montana 59870
Phone: 406-777-2729

DEDICATION

A hunter could not ask for better parents than my father, Stanley, and mother, Margaret. Their years of thoughtful guidance and persistent encouragement were the guiding spirit that made this tremendous task seem small. Thank you Mom and Dad.

The author is shown here with a limit of chukar in one of Oregon's best chukar hunting areas, along the Snake River.

Table of Contents

Dedication . . . . Page 5
Introduction . . . . Page 9
Chapter 1 — Roosevelt's Elk . . . . Page 13
Chapter 2 — Rocky Mountain Elk . . . . Page 27
Chapter 3 — Blacktail Deer . . . . Page 37
Chapter 4 — Mule Deer . . . . Page 49
Chapter 5 — Antelope . . . . Page 50
Chapter 6 — Black Bear . . . . Page 71
Chapter 7 — Bighorn Sheep . . . . Page 85
Chapter 8 — Cougar . . . . Page 95
Chapter 9 — Upland Birds . . . . Page 101
Chapter 10 — Waterfowl . . . . Page 131
Chapter 11 — Varmints . . . . Page 141
Chapter 12 — Bowhunting . . . . Page 153
Appendix A — Hunting Regulations . . . . Page 171
Appendix B—Extra Edge: Sources of Information . . . . Page 175

The author with an average 5-point bull taken in the Tioga unit near Reedsport, Oregon. Rifle used was a Ruger 350 Remington Magnum.

Introduction

The idea to write a book about Oregon hunting was spawned high atop a rugged mountain in the John Day River drainage of central Oregon. It was mid-October and the end of a marvelous mule deer hunt for our entire hunting party. We had drifted the same 15 miles of picturesque river five years in a row and arrived at the same camp we now call "home." The entire party had all taken nice bucks and the mood around camp was festive to say the least. Like the rest, I was happy but wanted to be alone and enjoy the solitude of a desert sunset, relive every detail of the hunt, and try to extend this Oregon wilderness experience as long as possible.

With my back resting against a weather-worn juniper and my feet propped on a volcanic rock formation, I watched the setting sun and thought of my good fortune and how much I really enjoy the out-of-doors. I thought about the great pleasure that hunting has brought into my life. It is fortunate indeed to live in a state with such diverse habitat and great hunting opportunity.

In Oregon the game is abundant and accessibility is tremendous throughout the state. The Beaver State is fairly large — nearly 62 million acres. The U.S. Government, mostly the Bureau of Land Management and the U.S. Forest Service, owns and manages 53% of the land in Oregon. State and local governments manage another 3%. That means that resident and nonresident hunters have access to over half of all the land in the state. In addition, most of the waters are publicly owned. Much of the remaining private land can be hunted by taking the time and courtesy to ask for permission to trespass. Most ranchers are more than willing to share their bountiful game with responsible hunters.

The quantity and variety of huntable game in Oregon is truly remarkable. Big game, small game, varmints, upland and migratory gamebirds are all there for the taking. The Oregon Department of Fish and Wildlife is one of the most progressive conservation agencies to be found in this nation. Good hunting will be around for generations to come thanks to them.

As I sat atop my castle in the fading sunset, I thought of how lucky I was and how much I had to be thankful for. For the price of a hunting license, the proper tags and a little gasoline, the entire state and year-round hunting pleasure was mine. Many hunters now-a-days take what we have here in Oregon for granted and do not seem to appreciate it.

Milo Raichl, a long time friend and Czechoslovakian immigrant who escaped from a German prison camp in World War II, is a supreme hunter. He expresses my feelings about the privilege of Oregon hunting as he describes the hunt on which he killed the former world record Roosevelt's elk. It was shot on my father's ranch along the Necanicum River near my hometown of Seaside, Oregon back in 1959. Taken directly from Boone and Crockett Club's 18th Big Game Awards Book for 1980-82, his story is as follows:

"I came to green Oregon from my former home in Czechoslovakia, where in my youth I had been a forestry man and a game warden. Now escaped from Communist oppression, I sought here peace, and memories of the green home I had left. An ardent hunter, I was delighted with the beauty and bounty of this lovely land full of trophy game, especially the Roosevelt's elk, the 'king of the forest.'

"On the first hunting day of November 1959, I was only four miles from my own house, in the Saddle Mountain area of Clatsop County, near the North Fork of the Necanicum River. I had my Enfield 303 rifle, with 220 grain Norma cartridges. Being in Western Oregon, we had just had plentiful rain but none was falling now. Snow was visible at about the 2,000 foot level of Saddle Mountain's 3,283 feet. The soft ground made for easy, quiet cold tracking.

"For a long time I had known about the large herd of Roosevelt's elk here, and I had admired the great bull with his whitish antlers and huge, bulky body. It didn't take long for me locate them, for you could hear and smell them long before they were visible. Even in thick brush, when they are quiet, they can be located by the steam rising from their great bodies.

"The herd was moving slowly, and I followed them quietly for about a quarter-mile along the North Fork of the Necanicum, toward the 300-400 Line road of the Crown Zellerbach Tree Farm. I had not taken a pickup on this hunt, for at that time, in this location, there were no good roads. It was the old, hard-time hunt on foot.

"Presently, I came up to the herd. With my old Enfield at the ready, I started looking for 'my' bull. With a good front wind, the herd didn't sense that I was near them, behind a huge, overgrown stump, searching for 'my'

trophy. Already, I felt he was mine although I hadn't seen him yet. With the trained eyes of a hunter, sharpened by too many years of bitter war, I watched the herd grazing the side of the hill before me. Not counting, just watching, I estimated between 50 and 60 elk in the herd.

"Finally, he stepped into view with his lovely white antlers and beautiful black neck, standing perhaps 60 yards ahead of me, close to a small creek.

"How quick and easy it was. My firm hand did not tremble when I lifted the old British army rifle and took aim at the beauty before me. 'Diana, please be my patron and let my bullet go directly into the heart of this majestic animal, that he may not suffer.' The old hunters' prayer was my last thought as I squeezed the trigger.

"The sound of the shot seemed to have frozen the herd for a moment, and the black necks moved the heads to face me as the huge body of my trophy crashed to the ground. What a triumphant feeling, known only to the hunter who has experienced it, and impossible to describe to one who has not. 'Thank you Diana, and St. Hubert too!' Pagan goddess and Christian saint, we hunters take help where we can get it. That moment will be with me for all my life.

"Now the hard work of the hunt lay before me. Before it was over, I would spend the better part of three days packing the animal out the four miles to my home. The work was very demanding and I was exhausted.

But, I am still proud that it was all done the proper way. There was no waste.

"While I was skinning my trophy, a forester from Crown Zellerbach Company came to the scene and congratulated me. He had probably been after the same bull. We both tried as hard as we could to estimate the live weight. An Oregon Department of Fish and Wildlife booklet reports that the bull Roosevelt's elk grows to a maximum of 1,300 pounds. But I believe, and the forester agreed with me then, that this bull was close to 1,700 pounds, with 1,780 pounds as the top estimate as it lay on the ground in front of us.

"What a huge animal! And what a lucky new citizen of my new land, Oregon and America, where anyone can go hunt for a small amount of money. In Europe, hunting is a privileged pleasure for the few who can afford it. Even today, some rich Americans are going to Communist Czechoslovakia to hunt West European stag or Carpathian elk, paying up to $2,000 for one shot, hit or miss. Here the fee is only $25.00 for a resident and we don't have to travel across the sea. I am saddened to think of how little appreciation some hunters have for this privileged land, how they waste the game and trophies, the thrill and the beauty. But I know, and care, and I shall be happy hunting in Oregon forever, with friends who care."

That evening, high above the John Day River, I felt compelled to write this book. The purpose is not to encourage huge numbers of local and out-of-state hunters to take to the field and overrun the countryside, but to instead encourage present-day hunters and future generations to appreciate the superior hunting opportunities we have here in Oregon. Through sound wildlife management and promotion of conservation and good hunting ethics, Oregon's fine hunting will last for years to come. I would like my son, his son and his son to reap the pleasures of Oregon's true treasure — the wildlife experience.

John A. Johnson
Reedsport, Oregon

Chapter 1

ROOSEVELT'S ELK

The November wind was in my face as I fumbled through the rain-soaked darkness. I caught the distant odor of elk and froze. The gray dawn revealed a herd of at least 30 animals browsing at timber's edge, no more than 150 yards away.

I had tracked this herd off and on for two days, rewarded only with an occasional glimpse of their yellow rumps as they disappeared in the dense salal and salmonberry thickets. Call it luck or an elk hunter's intuition, but my hunch was that the herd would be feeding near this small mountain meadow just at day break...

...and there they were!

It seemed like hours, but within minutes the entire herd was plainly visible. I frantically switched my scope from one animal to another hoping to find a legal bull. No such luck. They were all cows and calves except for three spikes, not legal in the Tioga unit of western Oregon. The herd bull I had watched all summer had fallen victim to another lucky hunter, and this was the last day of the short four day season.

Just then the wind shifted and the entire herd started trotting toward the dense timber. Suddenly, from out of the alders about 75 yards to the right of the herd, an ivory-tipped bull appeared. He held his head high as he tried to catch the scent of whatever had spooked his companions. It was a sight to behold as he walked stiff-legged back and forth not more than 150 yards in front of me.

The moment all elk hunters dream about was here. The crosshairs of my 3 power seemed to center automatically behind his near shoulder as I squeezed the trigger. A spray of moisture appeared above his neck as the 250 grain Hornady from my Ruger .350 Remington Magnum slammed into him. He leaped high indicating a heart hit, trotted a few yards, and dropped.

Eric Johnson, author's son, with a good Roosevelt's bull taken in the Tioga unit near Loon Lake. Rifle used was a Ruger 270.

The Number Three Boone & Crockett Roosevelt's elk was killed by Fred Williamson in Clatsop County, Oregon, in 1947. It scored 378 5/8 points. (Photo courtesy Rusty Lindberg.)

Somehow it seemed appropriate that this should be my best bull in 16 seasons. It was the eighth bull I had taken but the thrill felt just as it did the day I killed my first spike in Clatsop County when I was 16.

A mature Roosevelt bull is truly an impressive trophy. In general, they have shorter, more massive antlers and a 20% larger body size than Rocky Mountain elk of the same age. Roosevelt appear robust and compact, rather than long and rangy like Rocky Mountain elk. An average, mature Oregon Roosevelt bull will average about 775 pounds on the hoof and will have a dressed out weight of about 450 pounds — big animals!

Technically, Roosevelt elk inhabit the Coast-Range and the west slope of the Cascade Mountains. However, any elk to the east of the I-5 Freeway is a Rocky Mountain variety according to Boone and Crockett standards. In the lower 48 states, only Oregon and Washington have huntable populations of Roosevelt's elk. The most recent estimates places Oregon's Roosevelt's elk population at 59,000.

There have been anywhere from 45,000 to 55,000 Roosevelt's elk hunters in Oregon in recent years. They annually harvest from 4,000 to

6,000 elk with about 20% of the kill being antlerless animals. Bowhunters take about 10% of the total kill each year. The overall success rate runs about 10% in recent years.

The Saddle Mountain hunting unit on the north coast and the Tioga, Chetco, and Sixes units on the south coast are managed for three point or better bull harvest. Spike bulls, with antlers longer than the ears, are legal in all other units. Oregon has a split general rifle season for westside elk. The first season usually starts the first weekend in November and is four days long. The second season begins the following weekend and usually lasts a full week.

WHERE TO HUNT

The north coast has more Roosevelt's elk than any place in the state and, of course, more hunters. The Saddle Mountain, Trask and Wilson units produce the bulk of the kill.

On the south coast, the Tioga unit has the best elk habitat and consistently produces the vast majority of animals taken. According to Oregon Department of Fish and Wildlife district wildlife biologist Bill Hines, the Powers and Melrose units also yield fair numbers each year.

The Cascade area has fine Roosevelt habitat and has a fair elk population. Biologist Al Polenz says the bull/cow ratio in the Cascades is increasing after a single October season was adopted in 1986. The Indigo, Santiam, Rogue and McKenzie units are best bets.

TROPHY ROOSEVELT ELK

Oregon, without a doubt, has the finest hunting for trophy Roosevelt's elk in the world. At this writing, the Boone and Crockett Club lists 66 Roosevelt's elk that meet the minimum score of 290 points. Almost two-thirds (43) of those trophies have come from Oregon including 7 of the top 10 listings.

Approximately 90% of Oregon's trophy Roosevelt have come from three counties in the extreme northwestern corner of Oregon: Clatsop, Columbia, and Tillamook. The largest number of Boone and Crockett bulls came from Columbia County (15) with Clatsop (14) and Tillamook (9) close behind. The top three Oregon Roosevelt bulls ever listed have come from Clatsop County.

The current world record Roosevelt was killed by Robert Sharp in Clatsop County in 1949. The score was an impressive 384 3/8 with 9 points on the right beam and 8 on the left. It has an inside spread of 41 1/8 inches.

The Boone and Crockett Club officially recognized the Roosevelt's elk in 1980. Only those trophies found west of I-5 are considered Roosevelt; all others are listed as the Rocky Mountain variety. Because Roosevelt are

The current world record Roosevelt's elk was shot by Bob Sharp in Clatsop County, Oregon, in 1949. Boone and Crockett minimum score is 290 and this bull scored 384 3/8. Approximately two-thirds of the record-book Roosevelt's elk have come from Oregon.

The lush greenery of western Oregon provides excellent forage for the Roosevelt's elk. (Photo courtesy John Smart)

a relative newcomer to the Boone and Crockett Record Book, many more listings are expected to surface in the near future.

The field judging of a Roosevelt's trophy qualities can be a difficult chore. Roosevelt's elk have compact antlers which are smaller but more massive than those of its cousin, the Rocky Mountain elk, even though body size is larger. A really big Roosevelt's elk rack will appear less mature due to the compactness of the rack and overall larger body size. The basic points to look for when evaluating a potential trophy are long main beams of four feet, major points exceeding 12 inches, and an inside spread of at least three feet. Most high scoring Roosevelt bulls have the unique "crown" points, a characteristic of westside elk. If, when viewed from behind, a bull's antlers easily clear the body by a half foot margin on each side, the hunter is looking at a trophy elk.

HOW TO HUNT

A particular hunting style is necessary to be consistently successful when chasing Roosevelt elk in the lush green rain forests of western Oregon. There are a few basic hunting hints I've learned from hunter interviews and personal experience that can help any hunter to greater success on these huge deer.

Early scouting pays off. Your chances for taking a bull will be greatly improved if you spend a week or more finding herds and learning their habits. Roosevelt, unlike their eastside cousins, are rather territorial and have a limited home range. If you scout a herd before the season, chances are good the same herd will be no more than a mile from where you located them earlier.

Hunt remote timber away from roads. Many elk are shot each year by road hunters, but timber hunting provides a more satisfying experience as well as a better chance for a big bull according to Jack Himebaugh who has taken about 20 Roosevelt bulls in the Tioga unit. If you see more than one or two other people during a day's hunt, it is probably time to look for a more isolated area. Good elk timber is getting harder to find as logging activity increases. Rusty Lindberg from St. Helens, Oregon, is a noted authority on Roosevelt's elk, an official Boone and Crockett measurer, and excellent elk hunter with over 20 bulls to his credit. The vast majority of his bulls were collected while hunting the deep timber.

Find ideal habitat. Ideal Roosevelt elk habitat has several ingredients: old-growth or second-growth timber at least 20 years old, a clearcut or two within their home range, one or more creek bottoms with good stands of alder and salmonberry brush, and of course, a lot of elk sign. Hunting the best looking elk habitat won't do you a bit of good unless you find sign that indicates elk are present.

Western Oregon elk hunters who are consistent hunt the brush. This spike bull was killed in Clatsop County two miles from any road. Rifle used was a Winchester model 70 in 270.

An elk hunter glassing for elk in western Oregon. Roosevelt's elk thrive in clearcut logging areas as long as adequate escape cover has been left.

Follow the fresh tracks. I recently talked with an elk hunter who said, "I only track lone animals. The big bulls don't stay with the herd." Ron Greenwood, a superb coastal elk hunter from Reedsport, once explained to me that younger bulls will often stay with the herd and older bulls will also follow the main herd but stay 100 to 300 yards off to one side.

If you do locate a herd that appears to have no legal bulls, be sure to examine the surrounding area closely. I was timber hunting several season ago when I came across fresh tracks and started the tedious job of tracking. Within an hour, I came upon the entire herd, but no legal bull. Disappointed, I staggered off in the opposite direction but stopped when I heard a limb break. I looked up to see a fine four point bull that was just as surprised as I. I downed that bull at 40 yards and learned a valuable lesson.

Hunt slowly. Most Roosevelt hunters who are new at the game try to "bust-a-gut" and cover as much territory as possible. As they become seasoned elk hunters, they learn to slow down, be quiet and hunt cautiously. Helen Leach, a Douglas County resident and good elk hunter explained, "I always hunt slow and try to see or hear them first." Following her own advice, Helen has taken around a dozen bulls and still hunts elk even though she is over 70 years of age.

Be prepared to hunt all day. Oregon elk seasons are short and the best elk hunters will hunt from daylight until dark. It is a good idea to carry a small daypack with adequate food and other essentials to allow an all day hunt. In addition to plenty of lightweight food, a pack should include a knife, small hatchet, 50 feet of nylon cord, and waterproof matches. An eight foot square plastic tarp, small flashlight, and change of socks are also useful. This may seem like a lot to carry, but the entire pack weighs under five pounds and allows the hunter to be afield all day and, if necessary, all night. I once killed a bull about three miles from the nearest road and darkness fell just as I finished gutting him. Having no choice, I had to stay. However, I was prepared and remained semi-comfortable until morning.

Wear appropriate clothing. Hunting attire will vary with the weather conditions and the area you intend to hunt, but rain gear is essential when westside elk hunting. It is a good idea to wear wool top and bottom. It is quiet and will keep you warm even when wet. For heavy rain, try to find a rain jacket and pants made of material that "breathes"; traditional rain gear is far too bulky and gets hot when hunting is hard.

Good hunting boots are more than just a good idea; they are a necessity. For dry weather, Vibram-soled leather boots are great. The new lightweight Danner boots are excellent. For wet weather, many elk hunters use well-greased leather logger boots or caulks. I use rubber caulk boots, which are quite heavy but completely waterproof.

Choose the right caliber. We have all heard stories about the ability of elk to absorb lead and keep on going. Unquestionably, a large bull is a tough critter. However, I believe their ruggedness has been somewhat exaggerated. I've killed five bulls with a .270 using 130 grain handloads and the former world record Roosevelt was killed with a 303 British. Many elk have been killed with the 30-30, and I know a hunter with many bulls to his credit who only shoots a .257 Roberts.

I am not trying to say that these lighter calibers are best. They will kill elk in the hands of a good shot under ideal circumstances. The problem is most hunters are far from good shots and ideal conditions are rare in Roosevelt hunting. Quite often the only shot at a fine trophy is a rearend or flank shot as the bull is disappearing in heavy brush. Here you want a bullet that has enough weight and proper construction to reach the vitals. Calibers such as the 338, 350 Remington Magnum and 35 Wheland are great for this. The 7MM Remington Magnum, 30-06 and other 30 caliber magnums are definitely adequate provided bullets of heavy construction are used. My personal choice for the best all-round elk rifle is the 338 Winchester Magnum.

Get in shape. Mental as well as physical conditioning are as important in Roosevelt's elk hunting as is the rifle you use or the boots you wear. Mentally you must prepare yourself for those disappointing days when tracks are all you will find, or when after miles of following a lone elk, you come upon two lucky hunters who have killed your bull as it walked into a clearcut.

Physically you must be prepared for endless miles of elk trails winding through rain-soaked underbrush, not to mention being fit for the pack-out after your trophy is down.I once came upon a rugged-looking elk hunter as he was skinning out a big bull that was miles from the nearest road on the last day of the season. He was soaked to the skin and his clothes were far from clean. My first words were, "Man you sure are lucky!"

He slowly looked up and said, "This was anything but luck," and went back to skinning. After years of elk hunting, I now know what he meant. Luck plays a small role in the game of consistently successful elk hunting.

VIEWING AREAS

The Oregon Department of Fish and Wildlife developed an excellent elk viewing area where the public can see Roosevelt's elk in their natural surroundings. The Jewell Meadows Wildlife Area is over 1,000 acres in size and is located 12 miles west of the Sunset Highway near the community of Jewell in Clatsop County. It has an average resident elk population of around 300 animals. Over 70,000 people visit this elk viewing facility each year.

The Deans Creek elk viewing area is located five miles east of Reedsport on Highway 38 in Douglas County. This Roosevelt's elk viewing area is in the early stages of development and plans are incomplete at this writing. At present, viewers can observe 50 to 100 elk on any given day. However, plans are to manage the area for a maximum of 100 head of elk in the future.

The Jewell and Dean's Creek elk management areas are utilized and truly appreciated by all who take the time to view these magnificent animals. I've been entertained for endless hours, watching elegant bulls strut gracefully among the harems of cows and calves they try to possess. Hardly a car that passes by can resist a short stop to see what many people have never seen — native coastal elk in natural habitat.

ROCKY MOUNTAIN ELK FOUNDATION

This seems like the proper place to mention the fine work completed in Oregon by the Rocky Mountain Elk Foundation. This active organization is based out of Missoula, Montana, and is dedicated to the future of elk across the North American continent. They believe the elk resource is a heritage that sportsmen everywhere must cherish and manage wisely or lose. Here are some of their accomplishments in Oregon. They helped found the Western States Elk Workshop in Oregon in 1986, provided funds for the Siskiyou Elk Transplant Program in 1986, provided funds for meadow rehabilitation in the Siskiyou National Forest in 1987, and donated funding to develop the Dean's Creek elk viewing area in 1987.

1986 GENERAL ELK SEASON BY HUNT PERIOD

Units by Area or Zone	FIRST PERIOD HUNT RESULTS				SECOND PERIOD HUNT RESULTS			
	Total Hunters	Percent of Hunters	Bulls Harvested	Percent Hunter Success	Total Hunters	Percent of Hunters	Bulls Harvested	Percent Hunter Success
Scappoose	1,071	61	96	9	698	39	24	3
Saddle Mountain	1,661	64	274	16	935	36	66	7
Wilson	4,224	58	361	9	3,105	42	229	7
Trask	3,057	52	241	8	2,828	48	181	6
Stott Mountain	662	54	60	9	566	46	48	8
Alsea	1,733	57	96	6	1,288	43	96	7
Siuslaw	915	59	24	3	626	41	36	6
Willamette	554	77	12	2	168	23	12	7
NORTH COAST AREA	**13,877**	**58**	**1,164**	**8**	**10,214**	**42**	**692**	**7**
Tioga	2,081	63	351	17	1,200	37	131	11
Sixes	42	65	3	7	23	35	2	9
Powers	842	51	12	1	806	49	36	4
Chetco	24	52	0	0	22	48	1	5
Applegate	48	100	0	0	0	0	0	0
Evans Creek (Cascade Season)	312	100	0	0	– NO SEASON –			
Melrose	205	65	12	6	108	35	12	11
SOUTHWEST AREA	**3,554**	**58**	**378**	**11**	**2,537**	**42**	**182**	**7**
Santiam (Cascade season)	4,685	100	132	3	– NO SEASON –			
Metolius " "	60	100	0	0				
McKenzie " "	3,423	100	108	3				
Upper Deschutes " "	517	100	0	0				
Indigo " "	2,919	100	108	4				
Fort Rock " "	120	100	0	0				
Dixon " "	2,967	100	96	3				
Sprague " "	12	100	0	0				
Rogue " "	3,015	100	96	3				
Keno " "	697	100	24	3				
CASCADES AREA	**18,415**	**100**	**564**	**3**				
ROOSEVELT ELK TOTALS	**35,846**	**74**	**2,106**	**6**	**12,751**	**26**	**874**	**7**

Courtesy Oregon Department of Fish & Game

This herd of Roosevelt's elk located at the Dean's Creek Elk Viewing Area near Reedsport provides a unique viewing experience. (Photo courtesy John Smart)

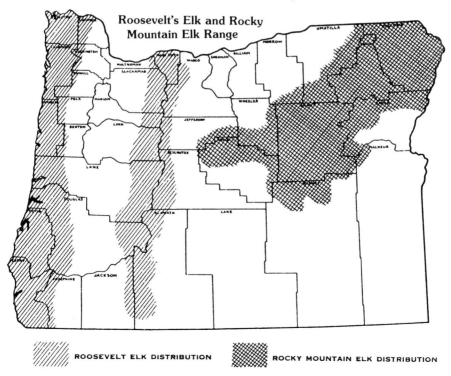

Roosevelt's Elk and Rocky Mountain Elk Range

ROOSEVELT ELK DISTRIBUTION   ROCKY MOUNTAIN ELK DISTRIBUTION

Jim Sproul with the largest Rocky Mountain elk ever taken in Oregon. It was shot in Grant County in 1972, and currently ranks 12th in the world with a Boone and Crockett score of 401 3/8. It has the longest main beams of any elk ever taken, with both measuring over 60 inches.

Chapter 2

ROCKY MOUNTAIN ELK

The greatest Rocky Mountain elk ever killed in Oregon was shot by James T. Sproul in Grant County in 1972. It has the longest main beams of any elk ever taken in the world with both beams measuring over 60 inches. It scored 401 3/8 Boone and Crockett points and currently ranks Number 13 in the world. Jim Sproul's story of how he took this majestic trophy is as follows:

"It was the second day of elk season in 1972. We left our ranch house before dawn with the temperature at 20 degrees F. and there was three inches of new snow on the ground — perfect for elk tracking. There was Denny Moore, his son Mike Moore, my dad and myself.

"We decided to hunt close to the ranch in an area that we knew well and try to cut some fresh tracks. It was an either-sex area at the time and we gave no thought as to whether it was a bull or a cow. We just wanted an elk. After about a half hour of driving around, we cut the tracks of what looked to be a yearling elk. Mike and I were the youngest, so we were elected to follow the tracks.

"On the first part of the hunt, Mike made a huge circle to get ahead and I followed the track — that's our usual procedure. After following the track for about a half mile, I came upon Mike. We decided that he'd follow track and I'd cut a circle. I'd just left Mike and gone about 200 yards up a real steep shale ridge when I heard what sounded like a man crunching snow around the hill. Thinking it was Mike, I decided to meet him. I took about three steps and decided the noise was being made by an animal and a big one coming my way.

"I saw the antlers first at about 80 feet. As he came into sight all I could think was 'My God, it looks like a set of elk antlers on a deer.' The huge rack was totally out of proportion with the body. He finally stepped out into the open at about 60 feet and tried to wind me as he had just seen my tracks. I was shooting a Model 88 Winchester in .284 with iron sights. The big bull started trotting broadside and my first shot broke his back. Two more and he was finished. Mike heard the shots and came running. All we could do was stand there open-mouthed for about five minutes. Mike finally spoke and said, 'This has got to be the biggest Rocky Mountain elk ever.' We gutted the bull out and went back to the ranch house to get the horses.

"We later had the bull measured officially and it scored 401 3/8. It was a six by seven. Had it been an even seven, it would rank in the top three of the world. At that time it ranked Number 11 in the world, and was the largest Rocky Mountain elk ever killed in Oregon."

The Rocky Mountain elk is an imposing game animal that varies in size according to sex, age, and area. A mature bull has six points on each antler, shoulder height is 4 1/2 or 5 feet, length is 7 1/2 to 9 feet, and weighs anywhere from 500 to 1,000 pounds on the hoof.

Bulls drop their enormous antlers by March and begin to develop new ones within a month. By July or early August, the fully developed velvet-sheathed antlers of a large bull may weigh 50 pounds. As a rule, older yearlings develop sizable spikes; two and three-year-olds display four and five tines on each beam. The next year's antlers have six long points on each massive beam. Generally, Rocky Mountain elk have larger antlers but a somewhat smaller body size that a Roosevelt's bull of the same age.

In general, Oregon's Rocky Mountain elk are found in the central and northeast sections of the state. The population of eastside elk in Oregon is estimated to be 56,000, almost identical to our Roosevelt's elk numbers.

Between 60,000 and 80,000 Oregonians hunt Rocky Mountain elk each year. They annually take between 10.000 and 16,000 elk. However, 30 to 50% of the total kill are antlerless. Because of this relatively high antlerless harvest, hunter success rates run high — 15 to 20%. Bowhunters usually account for less than 10% of the total kill.

The Snake River unit in the extreme northeastern portion of the state has a three point regulation and is limited entry. Spike bulls with horns longer than the ears are legal in all other units. Eastern Oregon has a split season and hunters must select first or second season. The first season is four days in length and usually begins the last weekend in October. The second season is seven days in mid-November.

WHERE TO HUNT

The northeastern section of the state has a large elk population, few hunters, and high hunting success with bull hunters averaging around 15%. The area consists of 12 hunting units, most of which have good numbers of elk and fair hunter success. According to Oregon Department of Fish and Wildlife's most recent data, the five best units in terms of bulls

Rocky Mountain bull elk. (Photo courtesy Dale A. Burk)

A mature Rocky Mountain bull is an impressive trophy. This monster was taken by Keith Whitehead with a model 94 Winchester in 30-30. (Photo courtesy Keith Whitehead)

1986 GENERAL ELK SEASON BY HUNT PERIOD

Units by Area or Zone	FIRST PERIOD HUNT RESULTS				SECOND PERIOD HUNT RESULTS			
	Total Hunters	Percent of Hunters	Bulls Harvested	Percent Hunter Success	Total Hunters	Percent of Hunters	Bulls Harvested	Percent Hunter Success
Minam	661	61	139	21	418	39	35	8
Imnaha	1,033	80	187	18	255	20	47	18
Catherine Creek	1,195	62	129	11	719	38	47	7
Keating	441	70	93	21	186	30	0	0
Pine Creek	1,056	88	244	23	139	12	12	9
Lookout Mountain	418	80	81	19	104	20	12	12
WALLOWA ZONE TOTAL	4,804	73	873	18	1,821	27	153	8
Snake River	485	55	111	23	395	45	60	15
Chesnimnus	– NO SEASON –				1,318	100	330	25
Sled Springs	2,808	79	219	8	731	21	47	6
Wenaha	2,483	88	419	17	336	12	59	18
Walla Walla	1,798	85	267	15	325	15	35	11
Mt. Emily	3,817	79	419	11	1,044	21	47	5
WENAHA-SNAKE ZONE	11,391	73	1,435	13	4,149	27	578	14
Starkey	5,592	80	592	11	1,439	20	104	7
Ukiah	4,757	72	499	10	1,856	28	140	8
Sumpter	4,316	72	302	7	1,671	28	162	10
Desolation	2,854	69	382	13	1,276	31	116	9
Heppner	5,174	78	568	11	1,462	22	151	10
Fossil	568	66	70	12	290	34	59	20
UMATILLA-WHITMAN ZONE	23,261	74	2,413	10	7,994	26	732	9
Northside	649	100	149	23	– NO SEASON –			
Murderers Creek	467	100	88	19				
Beulah	676	100	123	18				
Malheur River	367	51	38	10	351	49	67	19
Silvies	269	44	55	20	340	55	61	18
Ochoco	454	44	70	15	576	56	94	16
Grizzly	171	54	30	18	147	46	14	10
Maury	37	33	10	27	43	67	7	16
OCHOCO-MALHEUR ZONE	3,090	68	563	18	1,457	32	247	17
BLUE MOUNTAIN AREA TOTAL	42,546	73	5,284	12	15,421	27	1,706	11
Hood	139	60	0	0	93	40	0	0
White River	394	46	12	3	464	54	0	0
CENTRAL AREA	533	49	12	2	557	51	0	0
ROCKY MOUNTAIN ELK TOTAL	43,079	73	5,296	12	15,978	27	1,706	11

Courtesy Oregon Department of Fish & Game

Vintage photo of Rocky Mountain elk hunting the way it used to be. Old caption reads "Deer and elk — Pilot Rock, Oregon.

taken are in order as follows: Mt. Emily, Wenaha, Chesnimnus, Pine Creek, and Walla Walla.

The units more centrally located in the state have considerably more hunting pressure and a somewhat lower success rate. There are 14 hunting units. However, five of those units produce the bulk of the kill. In descending order, they are: Starkey, Heppner, Ukiah, Desolation, and Sumpter.

TROPHY ROCKY MOUNTAIN ELK

Five Oregon Rocky Mountain bulls have been entered in the Boone and Crockett Record Book which meet the minimum score of 375 points. Jim Sproul's great bull tops the list at 401 3/8 points from Grant County in 1972. The remainder are as follows: Lawton McDaniel (395 1/8) from Wallowa County in 1935, H.M. Bailey (389) from Umatilla County in 1963, Andy Chambers (387 4/8) from Grant County in 1959, and Pat Wheeler (380 3/8) from Harner County in 1967.

Any six point Rocky Mountain bull with symmetrical points is an impressive animal. A record book bull will have a long sweeping curve to the main beams that are five feet or more in length and have an inside spread of at least 40 inches. When viewed from the front, a record bull's antlers appear twice as wide as the body. When viewed from the rear, his antlers will clear the body by a foot or more. Although the imperial bull (7 points) is highly prized, most record book animals are Royals and have only six points.

HOW TO HUNT

There are basically three ways to hunt eastside elk: bugling, drive hunts, and stalking your bull.

Hunting Roosevelt's and Rocky Mountain elk is as different as day and night. Although heavy, lodgepole thickets are plentiful, in general Rocky Mountain elk are creatures of open expanses with far less brush than Roosevelt are accustomed to. Noisy rain, moist ground and dense brush often mask a hunter's approach when in pursuit of Roosevelt's elk. My experience is that Oregon's eastside elk are more wary and alert to a rifle hunter's approach than coastal elk. Air so crisp that sounds carry for miles and open terrain make clean stalks difficult.

Bugling for bulls is a thrilling and productive sport for the experienced hunter. Unfortunately Oregon's rifle season begins in October and continues into November, well beyond the rut. Only Bowhunters can take advantage of love-hungry bulls when their guard is down and they are extremely vulnerable.

Horses and successful Rocky Mountain elk hunting go hand in hand. They get you and your camp in and the meat and horns out. (Photo courtesy Keith Whitehead)

Eastside elk hunters should be prepared for snow in October and November.

A variety of bugles can be bought or made. The trick is to find one of sufficient length and diameter to simulate the four distinct tones of a bull elk's bugle. Buy a recording of the elk actually bugling and practice until you are confident.

Bugle only in locations with sufficient elk sign. Good places are canyon heads, high ridges and rim country. The best time to bugle is at sunrise. Bugle at 10 minute intervals and if there is no answer move on. Try every half mile or so. If a bull answers your call, sit tight for at least 30 minutes. Big bulls often approach silently from the opposite direction without a second answer.

Drives are conducted in canyons or small, fairly steep valleys where elk are known to frequent. Stands overlook clearings or open crossings where animals are likely to move out from the timber. Drivers move with the wind, hoping to keep animals ahead. One drawback of drives is that bulls may be so afraid that they break into a fast gallop and can reach speeds of 35 miles per hour — a tough target indeed.

Stalk hunting on foot is the most challenging way to hunt bull elk and provides the greatest sense of accomplishment should you connect. Normally, the game is located at long distance and stalking within rifle range is difficult to say the least. Once spooked, a Rocky Mountain bull will often continue flight for several miles — a spooked Roosevelt's bull will rarely range more than a half mile.

Stalking a lone bull can be a slow process. Elk habitat can be thick foliage and therefore quite noisy. A hunter must move slowly and utilize the terrain being careful never to "skyline" himself. Try always to see the bull before he sees you. Always try to approach from above and with the wind in your favor.

Keith Whitehead, from Tillamook, Oregon, is a longtime friend and one of, if not THE, best elk hunters in the state. Last season he killed his 30th bull elk and the majority have been the Rocky Mountain variety. His last six bulls have had antlers of six points and larger! He is unquestionably an elk hunter supreme.

I recently interviewed Keith in an effort to learn more about an expert's hunting methods and secrets to success. Some of his comments are as follows:

*The most important thing about Rocky Mountain elk hunting is the wind direction. Those elk depend on the wind to smell danger. Always approach downwind.

*Keep in mind when tracking lone bulls, that they make fresh trails and rarely stay on a main elk trail. They always seem to know if you are following them.

*A lone Roosevelt's bull has a limited home range and won't go too far. Rocky Mountain bulls will travel 10 to 12 miles per day when chased.

*I go fast, travel light and cover a lot of ground until I find sign or horn rubs. That tells me there is a bull near and then I go slow and hunt cautiously.

*Most of my elk have been killed with a Ruger 77 and 300 Winchester Magnum using 180 grain Hornady reloads. I use a 2 X 7 Leopold.

*Two reasons for my success are that I study maps over and over until I am familiar with the country. Also, I know my hunting partner well — usually it is my dad.

Keith still hunts with his father who is 75 years old and together they have accounted for 57 bull elk! Keith's advice is well worth trying.

Elk hunters must be prepared to hunt from daylight until dark and sometimes overnight. All of the equipment in this day-pack weighs less than three pounds.

Keith Whitehead is probably the best elk hunter in Oregon. At this writing, he has 30 bull elk to his credit. (Photo courtesy Keith Whitehead)

Blacktail buck. (Photo courtesy Oregon Department of Fish and Wildlife)

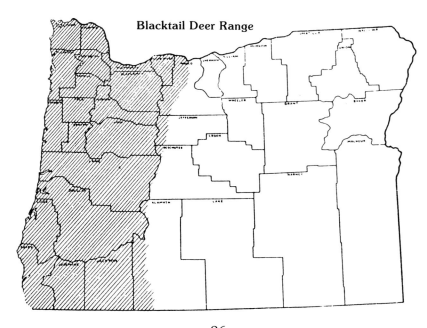

Blacktail Deer Range

Chapter 3

BLACKTAIL DEER

I sat on a large spruce stump that overlooked an enormous clearcut unit. My binoculars were glued to the timber's edge trying to penetrate the thick coastal fog. The evening prior I had seen a tremendous deer bouncing through the timber — it had to be a buck and I was hoping to catch him feeding at daybreak.

The morning was crisp and frosty with a white curtain of fog blanketing the entire unit. The silver cloud began to rise and within a short time I was glassing the entire canyon. As if this buck were destined to be mine, he suddenly appeared on a cat-road coming out of the timber. He wasn't more than 200 yards from where I had last seen him the evening before.

I took a steady rest with my Model 70 Winchester 270 and guessed the range at about 300 yards. The buck was facing me and looked like a big forked-horn as the crosshairs came to rest. I held for the center of his neck, knowing the 130 grain Nosler would drop into his chest if I had underestimated the range. I heard the slap after the shot and saw the buck rear high on his hind legs and then bolt into a small ravine.

My body seemed to glide as I ran over broken logs, small stumps, and huckleberry brush. His large tracks were easy to find and blood was everywhere. I began to track but hadn't covered 50 feet when the great buck leaped to his feet, exposing my off-center hit as he trotted past me. The next shot brought him down. His heavy antlers were much larger than I expected — 5 by 6. I guessed his weight at 160 pounds field dressed and he was in prime condition. On this occasion, patience and luck combined with an effective hunting technique produced a winter's meat supply and my best blacktail.

Blacktail deer are one of Oregon's most challenging and popular big game animals with from 60,000 to 150,000 hunters pursuing these evasive coastal deer each year. They harvest anywhere from 25,000 to 65,000 deer each year — antlerless deer comprise about one-third of the kill. Archers take about 10% of the total kill.

The blacktail is indeed a challenge to hunt and more difficult to take

This beautiful blacktail was shot by Dennis King in Jackson County. It scores 170 2/8 and ranks number five in the world.

than mule deer. The generally accepted geological boundary is western Oregon to the summit of the Cascade Mountains. In other words, the blacktail resides in the lush greenery and brushy terrain of western Oregon. These deer generally do not herd up as do mule deer, making them more difficult to spot. Also, these westside deer have the distinct characteristic of standing perfectly still when they sense a hunter is near. It is often nearly impossible to spot a deer "frozen" in this manner with proper cover. Blacktail are more difficult to see than mule deer as they do not have the large white rump patch as do muleys. Blacktail are a more wary and secretive animal than mule deer. I have done a considerable amount of big game hunting. I've lost track of the actual number of blacktail bucks that I have taken, but a dozen seems about right. I have been lucky enough to take my fair share of black bear, mule deer, and Roosevelt elk here in Oregon. In Alaska, I have successfully hunted Dall sheep, woodland caribou, Rocky Mountain goat, Kenai moose, and even the awesome Alaskan brown bear. Of all these big game species, it is my firm belief that a fully mature blacktail buck is one of the most difficult to bag — a real challenge.

Dennis King is one Oregon's premiere blacktail hunters. He has hunted them for over 30 years and taken five bucks that rank in the Boone and Crockett record book. All together, the King family has taken nine record book bucks. The largest buck was shot by Dennis in 1970 in Jackson

Blacktail like clearcut logging units and oftentimes will be found near the timber's edge.

This giant blacktail was shot by Clark Griffith in Lincoln County near Elk City, Oregon, in 1962. It scored 170 6/8 and was the world record for many years. Oregon ranks second only to California in numbers of bucks entered in the Boone and Crockett Club record book.

1986 BLACKTAIL DEER RIFLE SEASON

Units by Area or Zone	Hunters	General & Limited Entry Season: Buck Harvest	Hunter Choice Harvest	% Hunter Success	Subtotal Harvest	Subtotal Hunter Days	Controlled Hunters	Controlled Harvest	Controlled Hunter Days	Total Rifle Harvest	Total Hunter Days
Scappoose	4,331	710	460	27	1,170	32,291	0	0	0	1,170	32,291
Saddle Mountain	5,762	805	694	26	1,499	43,275	0	0	0	1,499	43,275
Wilson	3,878	595	337	24	932	26,350	0	0	0	932	26,350
Trask	9,831	1,209	1,150	24	2,359	72,937	0	0	0	2,359	72,937
Stott Mountain	3,485	485	386	25	871	25,835	0	0	0	871	25,835
Alsea	13,024	2,678	2,141	37	4,819	91,873	918	251	2,914	5,070	94,787
Siuslaw	6,074	1,023	435	24	1,458	45,872	0	0	0	1,458	45,872
Willamette	17,960	2,056	1,894	22	3,950	128,812	0	0	0	3,950	128,812
NORTH COAST AREA TOTALS	64,345	9,561	7,497	27	17,058	467,245	918	251	2,914	17,309	470,159
Tioga	5,953	1,368	0	23	1,368	46,093	861	447	5,653	1,815	51,746
Sixes	2,387	764	0	32	764	17,797	0	0	0	764	17,797
Powers	1,612	371	0	23	371	12,090	1,047	539	7,108	910	19,198
Chetco	2,478	719	0	29	719	20,761	337	227	3,119	946	23,880
Applegate	3,626	689	0	19	689	24,979	1,773	866	13,958	1,555	38,937
Evans Creek	3,787	721	0	19	721	31,102	1,309	661	9,295	1,382	40,397
Melrose	5,359	1,285	0	24	1,285	38,863	1,247	518	6,934	1,803	45,797
SOUTHWEST AREA TOTALS	25,202	5,917	0	23	5,917	191,685	6,574	3,258	46,067	9,175	237,752
Santiam	14,666	1,376	1,263	18	2,639	103,569	26	8	131	2,647	103,700
McKenzie	8,632	1,224	935	25	2,159	67,817	0	0	0	2,159	67,817
Indigo	3,173	762	0	24	762	23,923	1,274	635	7,530	1,397	31,453
Dixon	5,238	1,467	0	28	1,467	38,963	669	407	4,769	1,874	43,732
Rogue	12,490	2,373	0	19	2,373	95,518	647	321	4,896	2,694	100,414
CASCADES AREA TOTAL	44,199	7,202	2,198	21	9,400	329,790	2,616	1,371	17,326	10,771	347,116
Western Oregon Muzzleloader	0						963	565	4,981	565	4,981
High Cascades Buck	0						2,472	330	9,825	330	9,825
BLACKTAIL DEER TOTALS	133,746	22,680	9,695	24	32,375	988,720	13,543	5,775	81,113	38,150	1,069,833

Courtesy Oregon Department of Fish & Game

County. It currently ranks Number Five in the world, and scores 170 2/8.

When asked where blacktail rank among Oregon's big game trophies Dennis states, "A mature blacktail is unquestionably Oregon's most difficult big game. Guided hunts for mule deer, Roosevelt and Rocky Mountain elk and black bear are easy to come by, but few guides go after blacktail. They are smart animals and rarely leave the brush. We make drive hunts through brush patches while hunters watch the trails and that has been the secret to our success."

Adult Oregon blacktail bucks stand about 37 inches high, field-dress from 110 to 150 pounds, and rarely reach the 200 pound mark. They are considerably different in appearance from mule deer, which routinely dress out over 200 pounds. Blacktail have less prominent ears than mule deer and the entire surface of its upper tail is black. Both mule deer and blacktail have antlers similar in appearance. However, blacktail racks are usually much smaller. A coast buck's first antlers will almost always be spikes, whereas a mule deer will usually have forks.

WHERE TO HUNT

The blacktail deer harvest is fairly uniform throughout the Oregon coast and Cascade areas. However, there are a few locations worthy of mention. In the north coast, according to Oregon Department of Fish and Wildlife hunting statistics, the Alsea unit is the most productive followed in order by the Trask, Willamette, and Saddle Mountain units. Harold Sturgis is a district wildlife biologist for the Oregon Department of Fish and Wildlife and is considered Oregon's most respected authority on blacktail deer. When asked to pinpoint the best unit for blacktail, the biologist states, "The Alsea is my choice as the most productive unit in Oregon and annual hunting statistics bear that out. Each year more and more hunters participate, and hunter success remains stable." On the south coast, the Tioga unit generally has the highest harvest followed by the Applegate and Melrose units. In the Cascade area, the Santiam and Rogue units are best bets followed in order by the McKenzie and Dixon units.

If you are looking for a truly unique hunting experience try the Oregon sand dunes in the Tioga and Siuslaw units. These snow-white sand dunes stretch from the Siuslaw River estuary near Florence, southward to Coos Bay. Blacktail can be quite elusive in the wide open expanses of this mini-Sahara. There is little competition, breathtaking scenery, and good numbers of deer. A friend of mine, Dan Campbell of Winchester Bay, has taken 13 bucks from the sand dunes over the years.

TROPHY BLACKTAIL

For the trophy hunter, Oregon ranks second only to California in

A mature blacktail buck is a wary animal — possibly the most difficult big game trophy to bag in Oregon. This buck was shot near Reedsport. (Photo courtesy Jason Campbell)

numbers of bucks entered in the Boone and Crockett record book. Oregon's record book blacktail originate from at least 15 counties. Jackson County leads with 17 entries, but since many of those bucks were taken, deer in most of that county are not considered pure-blooded blacktail by the Boone and Crockett Club. Next is Douglas County with 15, Lane and Clackamas with seven each, and Linn and Marion with six each.

The current new record blacktail was shot by B.G. Shurtleff in Marion County in 1969. It has seven points on each side and scored 172 2/8 points. Prior to that, Clark Griffith had the largest blacktail in the book. It had five points on each antler, scored 170 6/8 points, and was taken in Lincoln County near Elk City.

HOW TO HUNT

Oregon blacktail live in a variety of habitat types from bleached white sand dunes of wind-swept ocean beaches and rain forests of northern Oregon, to snow-covered crags near the crest of the Cascade Mountains. Regardless of the habitat type you are hunting, there is one important fact

My brother, Stan, with a large forked-horn blacktail taken in steep country. Rifle is a Winchester model 70 in.270.

to remember — the average blacktail spends its entire life in an area no greater than one square mile and usually far less. The "Mediterranean" climate of western Oregon is relatively mild and deer are not forced into long migration patterns such as the mule deer of central and eastern Oregon. Keep this fact in mind and your chances of killing a cagey old buck are greatly improved.

The variety of hunting techniques is great indeed. They vary from hunter to hunter depending on the individual's physical condition, hunting savvy, and sense of sportsmanship. Of course the terrain and cover in the hunting area play an important role in the choice of hunting methods.

Timber hunting is the choice for those hunters who prefer seclusion and solitude and are part Indian at heart. Success or failure is to a large part dependent on your hunting skills. I like to hunt the timber adjacent to a fairly large clearcut where I have seen a lot of sign. Timber hunting is best during stormy days when the wind and rain help mask a hunter's approach.

Still-hunting is another tried and proven technique for blacktail. The idea is to find an area where deer are plentiful, take a good vantage point with a view of several hundred yards, and be patient. Many handicapped or physically impaired hunters prefer to still-hunt as little or no physical effort is required.

Hunting from a stand while others drive through a canyon has accounted for many blacktail. However, there are some drawbacks. Any time several people are hunting the same canyon, safety problems arise. Also, when other hunters see your group making a drive, oftentimes they will join right in hoping your party will "dog" a deer to them. Not good sportsmanship, but it happens.

A **deer call** is seldom used in Oregon, but it is a very effective way to lure blacktail bucks out of the brush during late season. My brother, Stan Johnson, lives in Sitka, Alaska, and has killed dozens of blacktail using a deer call. This method is routine in Alaska. However, I know only a few hunters here in Oregon who use deer calls. These sportsmen claim that it is a deadly hunting technique and have the racks to prove it. The high-pitched squeal apparently simulates a doe's estrus call during the rut. No doubt more coastal deer hunters will use calls when they find just how effective they really are.

SEASONS

Western Oregon general buck season offers much hunting opportunity with an approximate 30 day season. It normally begins the first weekend of October and continues into early November. A forked-horn or larger buck must be taken during general season. Traditionally the last five days of the season have been open for hunter's choice in designated units. In addition, permits are usually available for controlled deer hunts throughout western Oregon. These permits allow the hunter to take an additional spike or antlerless deer.

Western Oregon bowhunters are normally allowed about 30 hunting days during August and September and any deer may be taken. Be aware that bucks may have antlers still in the velvet at this time and some trophy hunters consider them less desirable in this condition.

Hunting blacktail in Oregon with a muzzleloader has recently become popular with those hunters who prefer close range and the thrill of taking a deer with a single shot. Some western Oregon muzzleloader hunts are available but opening dates and units vary from year to year.

A 30 day season should bring every blacktail hunter more success you would think. Blacktail bucks are wary game and the hunter who is not willing to climb those steep canyons, beat that timber or wait out his buck, will go without venison. I stand by my earlier statement that a mature blacktail buck is one of North America's most difficult game animals to bag. After you have collected several of these beauties, you will feel the thrill of being a very accomplished Oregon big game hunter indeed.

A blacktail deer hunting camp in Douglas County probably around 1920. (Douglas County Museum Photograph)

An exceptional blacktail taken near Coos Bay. (Photo courtesy Joe Hudson)

The largest typical mule deer ever taken in Oregon was shot by Dr. John Evans in Wallowa County in 1920. It scored 209 4/8 and ranks number 13 in the world. (Photo courtesy Weibel Taxidermy)

Chapter 4

MULE DEER

"Get up, the coffee's hot." Those were the first words I heard the opening morning of my first mule deer hunt. A friend and I had decided to try for muleys Friday afternoon and got a late start after work. We arrived about midnight on a logging road somewhere around 20 miles north of John Day, Oregon. We did not have a tent, so we just covered ourselves with a canvas tarp which was now crusted with heavy white frost. At 21, my friend was a veteran mule deer hunter with many bucks to his credit. I had hunted blacktail for about 10 years but was anxious to try mule deer hunting.

Coffee never tasted better as we huddled for warmth around that small "Indian fire" and I listened to helpful hints about mule deer hunting. A couple of pancakes each and we went our separate ways just as first daylight revealed pine and juniper covered mountains that were "steeper than a cow's face." All was blanketed in ice and the setting was magnificent.

I worked my way up the hillside through dense pine thickets all the while following a well-worn deer trail with plenty of tracks. On several occasions I jumped deer, but could only see their white rumps bouncing ahead. Finally I came to the top where the trees began to thin out with many small ravines dissecting the ridge I was on.

My eyes watered and my nose ran as I walked into the icy breeze. Everything was perfect and I fully expected to see a nice buck as I crept from one small canyon to the next. My enthusiasm began to fade after an hour or so — it seemed as though I was hunting high timber ghosts rather than mule deer. Tracks were everywhere but I couldn't see a deer. A couple more draws and I'd make my way back to camp.

I came to a large canyon and peered deep into its depths. There they were, a whole herd, maybe 20 animals and they had no idea I was around. No big bucks in this herd, but a nice forked horn finally appeared

Mule deer. (Photo courtesy Oregon Department of Fish and Wildlife)

in my binoculars just off to one side. I took a rest and started to squeeze the trigger when my hunting partners last words echoed in my ear, "Good luck John and remember, don't shoot the first forked horn you see. There's some nice bucks around here." It was a difficult decision, but I put the safety on and walked away.

About a half hour later I came to another enormous canyon that looked good. I was definitely having second thoughts about passing up that first buck as I sat down to glass the canyon. The stiff breeze was biting cold and I had difficulty with vision as my eyes continuously ran tears. Suddenly, I spotted a lone buck bedded at the end of a log only a couple steps away from a dense pine thicket. It looked like a nice buck, no question about it.

I laid my daypack down and rested my 270 Model 70 Winchester across it. I judged the range at 325 yards and knew I would get only one shot — he was fully aware of my presence. I held for the top of his back and squeezed off. I recovered from the recoil just in time to see him leap up and disappear into the trees. My heart sank as he showed no sign of a hit.

Out of habit, I decided to mark where he was laying, work my way across the canyon, and check for blood. I found his bed and there was an inch wide trail of near orange blood leading into the timber. That is characteristic of a good lung hit and I knew he wouldn't be far. Only a short distance and there he was, my first mule deer. He wasn't a trophy by

A nice mule deer taken in the Steens Mountains. This unit has been managed for 4-point or larger bucks in the past several years.

A 25-inch mule deer, such as this fine buck, is a good mule deer by Oregon standards.

mule deer standards, but larger in body than any blacktail I had ever taken. His rack was 23 inches wide, three points on each side, and field dressed about 180 pounds — a good buck by my standards.

Mule deer are a very popular animal to hunt in Oregon. According to Oregon Department of Fish and Wildlife statistics, 100,000 to 180,000 sportsmen hunt muleys on the east side of the Cascade Mountains each year. They take from 30,000 to 100,000 mule deer annually with antlerless deer typically representing 10 to 20% of the kill. Bow and arrow enthusiasts represent about 10% of the effort and harvest.

Mule deer are my favorite big game to hunt in Oregon for several reasons. They reside east of the Cascades in the drier portions of Oregon — camping in the rain is never fun. A week long camp-out in pine, juniper or sage scenery makes for a memorable hunting experience. They are large-antlered and heavy-bodied deer. It is not at all uncommon for a mature buck to have a 25 inch four point rack and field dress at well over 200 pounds. They are somewhat easier to hunt than blacktail in that they tend to run in herds and have a large white rump patch. Both of these characteristics make muleys easier to spot. In general, mule deer reside in more open country and do not have the blacktails tendency to "freeze" when a hunter is in the area. When hunted fair chase, Oregon mule deer hunting is a quality experience.

WHERE TO HUNT

Hunt anywhere east of the summit of the Cascade Mountains and you are in mule deer country. Oregon Fish and Wildlife records show that the central Oregon area produces the highest annual kill of mule deer and is the most popular area in terms of overall hunter days in the state. We are basically talking about the center of the state from the Columbia River on the north to the California border on the south. It includes the east side of the Cascades and plenty of juniper/sagebrush country. It takes more hunting effort to harvest a deer in the central Oregon area than any other due to the increased competition. The best units in terms of total deer taken are the Paulina, Silver Lake, Four Rock, and upper Deschutes.

The least popular area in Oregon for mule deer is the high desert zone of southeastern Oregon. It is a huge hunting area and with the exception of the Steens Mountains, it is dry desert and fairly flat country. Relatively few hunters venture to this rugged and remote part of the state. However, Oregon Department of Fish and Wildlife hunting figures show that hunter success is usually quite high. This is a good area to hunt for those who like little competition and plenty of walking ground. The Wagontire and Owyhee units are the best buck producers. The Steens Mountain unit is one of the most scenic and productive hunting units. However, it has been regulated as a "trophy" unit area with limited hunting access.

The Blue Mountain area is a good choice for mule deer hunters. This is

Even a young mule deer buck like this one can be considered a trophy when taken on foot, in tough terrain and miles from any road.

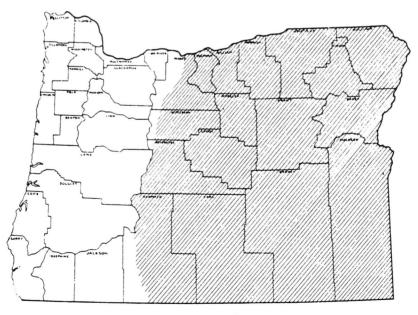

Mule Deer Range

Eric Johnson with a young mule deer shot near Service Creek in central Oregon. Rifle is a Ruger 270.

basically the northeastern portion of the state and includes the Blue and Ochoco Mountains and the Snake River Canyons. Vast stands of lodgepole pine, juniper and steep terrain characterize this country. The extreme northeastern section of the state had only limited hunting opportunity in recent years due to severe winter kill. It is recovering nicely at this writing and units such as Lookout Mountain, Keating, Mount Emily and Sled Springs will again yield good numbers of deer. Hunting pressure and deer harvest remain fairly uniform from year to year throughout the remainder of this area. Units that merit mention are Heppner, Fossil, Ochoco, Grizzly, and Beulah.

TROPHY MULE DEER

According to Rich LaRocco, past western field editor for Outdoor Life, Oregon ranks about midway in the list of states that have placed bucks in the Boone and Crockett record book. A total of 14 typical bucks and three nontypical bucks which came from 14 counties, are entered in the latest edition of Records of North American Big Game. The largest typical mule deer taken in Oregon was shot by Dr. John Evans in Wallowa County in 1920. It ranks 13 in the world, scores 209 4/8 points and has eight points on the left and six on the right beam. The largest nontypical mule deer ever taken in Oregon by a rifle hunter was shot by Bradley Barclay in Malheur County in 1971. This monster has a total of 38 points, scores 281 4/8 points and ranks 13 in the Boone and Crockett records book.

A quick glance at the record book shows that record mule deer can come from anywhere east of the Cascade Mountains. In very general terms, most of Oregon's record heads come from central and southeastern Oregon. Eldon Buckner is an official scorer for the Boone and Crockett from Baker, Oregon. He has probably scored more trophy antlers and come into contact with more mule deer hunters than anyone in Oregon. Mr. Buckner states "southeastern Oregon, especially around Jordan Valley, used to be where most of Oregon's trophy muleys came from. That is changing to northeastern Oregon. A bad winter kill forced the Oregon Department of Fish and Wildlife to close the season for several years and some huge bucks are now coming out of that country." In fact, Buckner has recently measured two heads from northeast Oregon that will be entered in the next edition of Boone and Crockett.

Because of the variation in size between areas, trophy mule deer are hard to estimate. One of the best ways to size up a trophy mule deer is to look for the amount of width between the antlers and the body as seen when the animal faces either head-on or away from the hunter. A deer is trophy sized if either antler overhangs the body by at least half the body width. Also, a trophy mule deer will have antlers at least one-half the animal's height from withers to the ground.

Julius Hopper, who lives and hunts the Huntington area on the Snake

1986 MULE DEER RIFLE SEASON

GENERAL AND LIMITED ENTRY SEASONS — CONTROLLED SEASONS

Units by Area or Zone	Hunters	General & Limited Entry Season Buck Harvest	Hunter Choice Harvest	% Hunter Success	Subtotal Harvest	Subtotal Hunter Days	Hunters	Harvest	Hunter Days	Total Rifle Harvest	Total Hunter Days
Minam	1,107	497	0	45	497	4,299	0	0	0	497	4,299
Imnaha	1,462	746	0	51	746	5,321	0	0	0	746	5,321
Catherine Creek	193	154	0	80	154	572	0	0	0	154	572
Keating	98	86	0	88	86	343	0	0	0	86	343
Pine Creek	28	21	0	75	21	86	0	0	0	21	86
Lookout Mountain	70	61	0	87	61	174	0	0	0	61	174
WALLOWA ZONE TOTALS	2,958	1,565	0	53	1,565	10,795	0	0	0	1,565	10,795
Snake River	412	193	0	47	193	1,800	0	0	0	193	1,800
Chesnimnus	1,140	638	0	56	638	4,108	0	0	0	638	4,108
Sled Springs	1,666	684	0	41	684	6,266	44	41	88	725	6,354
Wenaha	419	43	0	10	43	1,902	216	61	872	104	2,774
Walla Walla	1,774	480	0	27	480	7,311	0	0	0	480	7,311
Mt. Emily	2,258	655	0	29	655	9,376	0	0	0	655	9,376
WENAHA-SNAKE TOTALS	7,713	2,693	0	35	2,693	30,763	260	102	88	2,795	31,723
Starkey	162	94	0	58	94	652	0	0	0	94	652
Ukiah	4,053	1,257	0	31	1,257	17,158	288	199	712	1,456	17,870
Sumpter	279	231	-	83	231	978	95	87	152	318	1,130
Desolation	2,838	568	-	20	568	12,674	0	0	0	568	12,674
Heppner	5,881	1,590	0	27	1,590	28,448	1,044	712	2,799	2,302	31,247
Fossil	3,924	1,256	0	32	1,256	17,696	446	311	1,251	1,567	18,947
Columbia Basin	1,688	641	0	38	641	7,182	358	248	1,051	889	8,233
UMATILLA-WHITMAN ZONE TOTALS	18,825	5,637	0	30	5,637	84,788	2,231	1,557	5,965	7,194	90,753
Northside	1,995	811	0	41	811	9,741	306	128	978	939	10,719
Murderers Creek	2,131	1,012	0	47	1,012	9,643	0	0	0	1,012	9,643
Beulah	4,978	2,190	0	44	2,190	17,020	0	0	0	2,190	17,020
Malheur River	2,260	1,175	0	52	1,175	11,423	10	6	22	1,181	12,604
Silvies	2,277	1,109	0	49	1,109	10,826	0	0	0	1,109	10,826

Ochoco	18,031	2,087	0	26	2,087	35,554	1,070	823	3,189	2,910	38,743
Grizzly	3,623	1,052	0	29	1,052	14,858	1,525	1,022	3,667	2,074	18,525
Maury	1,172	422	0	36	422	4,817	460	387	1,024	809	5,841
OCHOCO-MALHEUR ZONE TOTALS	**26,467**	**9,858**	**0**	**37**	**9,858**	**113,882**	**3,371**	**2,366**	**8,880**	**12,224**	**122,762**
BLUE MOUNTAIN AREA TOTALS	**55,963**	**19,753**	**0**	**40**	**19,753**	**240,228**	**5,862**	**4,025**	**15,805**	**23,778**	**256,033**
Biggs	1,742	748	0	43	748	8,011	210	162	584	910	8,595
Maupin	613	172	0	33	172	2,366	91	58	241	230	2,607
Hood	1,054	126	0	12	126	4,582	88	17	503	143	5,085
White River	2,258	340	0	15	340	8,957	28	23	40	363	8,997
Metolius	1,903	552	0	29	552	9,773	336	304	640	856	10,413
Paulina	7,622	1,753	0	23	1,753	39,981	0	0	0	1,753	39,981
Upper Deschutes	6,913	1,453	0	21	1,453	33,511	0	0	0	1,453	33,511
Fort Rock	4,150	1,162	0	28	1,162	23,825	456	435	1,048	1,597	24,873
Silver Lake	4,494	1,258	0	28	1,258	25,803	448	399	1,048	1,657	26,851
Sprague	1,086	262	0	24	262	5,495	0	0	0	262	5,495
Klamath Falls	4,666	1,540	0	33	1,540	20,664	33	23	119	1,563	20,783
Keno	2,311	763	0	33	763	10,835	0	0	0	763	10,835
Interstate	3,118	1,123	0	36	1,123	16,160	0	0	0	1,123	16,160
Warner	2,236	1,007	0	45	1,007	9,847	0	0	0	1,007	9,847
CENTRAL AREA TOTALS	**44,166**	**12,259**	**0**	**28**	**12,259**	**219,810**	**1,690**	**1,421**	**4,223**	**13,680**	**224,033**
Wagontire	957	403	0	42	403	4,140	0	0	0	403	4,140
Beatys Butte	483	272	0	56	272	2,651	144	76	639	416	3,290
Juniper	319	148	0	46	148	2,056	0	0	0	148	2,056
Steens Mtn.	802	172	0	21	172	4,209	0	0	0	172	4,209
Whitehorse	664	321	0	48	321	3,035	0	0	0	321	3,035
Owyhee	1,516	758	0	50	758	6,774	86	68	122	826	6,896
HIGH DESERT AREA TOTALS	**4,741**	**2,074**	**0**	**44**	**2,074**	**22,865**	**230**	**144**	**761**	**2,286**	**23,626**
MULE DEER TOTALS	**104,870**	**34,086**	**0**	**33**	**34,086**	**482,903**	**7,782**	**5,590**	**20,789**	**39,999**	**503,692**

Courtesy Oregon Department of Fish & Game

The best place to find big mule deer bucks is in rugged country with limited access by man. This is the Snake River canyon and home to some exceptional bucks.

River, is undoubtedly one of the finest hunters in the state of Oregon when it comes to trophy mule deer. He is over 60, has hunted over 50 years, and has taken over 15 mule deer with spreads of over 25 inches and better. When asked to what he attributed his success, he replied, "If you want to take big bucks year after year, a hunter's got to learn to pass up the little ones. I remember years ago my 13-year-old son passed up 21 legal bucks opening morning and finally killed a big one later that season." It takes a lot of will power that many of us will never know, but big trophy Oregon mule deer are out there for the taking if we hunters will just take Hopper's proven advice.

HOW TO HUNT

The variety of habitat types where mule deer are found is truly amazing. From the snow fields and lodgepole thickets at the crest of the Cascades to juniper flats in central Oregon and endless golden slopes of the Snake River Canyon, muleys can be hunted virtually anywhere east of the Cascade Mountains. Select your preferred hunting area but remember one thing — mule deer are an adaptable animal and can migrate long distances.

The extreme weather variations in the eastern sector of the state force mule deer into short and long migrations to find food, water, and shelter.

Take the time to locate **the summer and winter range** of the specific deer you intend to hunt. According to Steve Denny, district wildlife biologist for Oregon Department of Fish and Wildlife, the summer range of mule deer is much higher in elevation than the winter range. Good mule deer hunters can predict with fair accuracy the elevation and habitat type where they expect to find deer during various weather patterns.

I know two hunting parties that recently hunted the Northside unit with contrasting degrees of success. The party with no prior hunting experience in that unit got skunked and came home with stories of hot and dry hunting conditions and poor deer management by the Oregon Department of Fish and Wildlife. The experienced hunters all came home with bucks and spotted many more. At first they hunted down low with no success. They moved camp 1,000 feet higher and found plenty of deer still on their summer range.

Much of central and eastern Oregon is high desert and wide open country. Vast sagebrush flats are difficult to hunt in that deer can see and hear a hunter's approach for miles in some cases. I prefer to **hunt the steeper terrain** with rimrock and broken topography. I try to get up high where the view is commanding and hunt just above rimrocks while looking down. Mule deer, especially the larger bucks, seem to find security just below large rimrocks and outcroppings. The best way to approach a buck that is bedded below these small cliffs is from above and on foot.

A tried and proven way to put mule deer venison in the freezer is to **hunt from a stand** that overlooks a well used deer trail leading to an irrigated alfalfa field. Lush, green alfalfa offers a welcome break from a muley's routine diet of bitterbrush and cheatgrass. Should you be lucky enough to obtain permission to hunt these "field" deer, chances for success are quite high if you hunt early morning and late evening. Although this situation does not provide the most sporting hunt and small and medium sized bucks are the rule, you will be rewarded with some of the best tablefare found anywhere.

Hunting from a stand is also productive if the brush is thick and dry and other hunters are active in the area. A friend came upon a tobacco-chewing, grizzled, old man several seasons ago who was just gutting a big buck on opening morning. My buddy complimented him on the trophy and started to move off when the old man said, "You want a buck just stay right here and let those crazies move em this way. I've killed at least 30 bucks over the years from this very knob." In less than an hour my partner had a three point with a 25 inch spread.

Some of Oregon's best mule deer hunting occurs on private property. In the past and even today, many landowners give permission to trespass to courteous hunters who take the time and effort to ask for it. For those unfortunates who do not ask and are apprehended while hunting on private property, criminal trespass is a serious offence and the penalties are severe indeed.

A good spotting scope is almost a necessity when the country is open and deer are spooky.

The Steens Mountains of southeastern Oregon not only has impressive scenery, but is one of the best areas in the state for trophy mule deer. (Photo courtesy Oregon Department of Fish and Wildlife)

Many eastside landowners are now allowing deer hunting only if the hunter is willing to pay for it. That statement no doubt raises the hackles of most hunters. However, **fee hunting** may not be as bad as it sounds. The fee charged is usually quite reasonable — $25.00 to $100.00 per gun or sometimes for the entire party. Fee hunting limits hunter numbers and improves hunting success. The rancher is familiar with his property and habits of the deer that use it. He will often share this knowledge with you which reduces scouting time. Fee hunting is here to stay and seems to be a growing trend. Hunters who would rather not pay to hunt can take heart in knowing they will always have a place to mule deer hunt — 56% of all Oregon land is in public ownership.

Oregon Department of Fish and Wildlife's staff biologist Ken Durbin and a good antelope. (Photo courtesy Oregon Department of Fish and Wildlife)

Chapter 5

ANTELOPE

"As I watched the big buck antelope run up the hill with several does in a serpentine pattern, the hunter I was guiding fired the last shot from his magazine. It was the fifth attempt and seventeenth .270 cartridge he'd fired at this same animal during the hunt and my heart sank as I watched a doe crumple a few feet beyond the buck. So ended one Oregon hunter's attempt at bagging a record class trophy during the 1980 season in eastern Oregon's Lookout Unit.

"The following year I drew a permit for this same area and the evening before the season opened I bedded down a few hundred yards from where this great buck and his harem had decided to spend the night. I didn't sleep well, feeling somewhat guilty about the imagined ease with which I would bag this buck with the heavy, narrow horns at daybreak. I need not have worried. Half an hour before light a pickup left the dirt road nearby and rattled cross-country up the flat, grassy draw where the herd had bedded. Needless to say, it scattered the antelope probably without those inside ever seeing them in the dark.

"Thoroughly frustrated, I set out on foot for another area a mile away where I had seen the buck before the season and arriving there, set up my spotting score in the sagebrush. I soon heard what sounded like the start of a Mexican revolution from north of the area I had come from. Within 15 minutes, I glassed five antelope trotting from the direction of the shooting I'd heard. As I watched, they picked their way off a low rim into a funnel-shaped sagebrush basin about 600 yards from me. I recognized the sole buck in this group as the one I'd bedded down the night before.

"The antelope had begun to settle down and were even beginning to feed a little when I heard the sound of a vehicle. Presently, two pickups appeared on a jeep road, then left it and drove cross-country into the upper end of the basin the antelope were in. As the vehicles continued down the bottom of the basin, the antelope saw them and began running, at which time they were spotted by the occupants of the vehicles who immediately gave chase. After shortening the range about 300 yards, the pickups stopped and at least two people fired at the fleeing pronghorns. I was surprised that none of the herd was hit as at least a dozen shots were fired. From my vantage point, I watched the antelope run in a big semicircle and finally come to a halt high up on a mountain slope over two miles away. I was relieved to see they were at last in an area where vehicles couldn't navigate, and packing up my scope, set out in their direction.

"By 9:00 a.m., some two hours later, the big buck and his greatly depleted harem of four does had moved down the mountain slope a half mile and were bedded down with about 15 other antelope, all does and fawns. I had hiked nearly three miles keeping track of the big buck and was some 500 yards from the bedded herd with no prospects of getting closer without being seen. As I lay watching in the broiling August sun, I noticed two more antelope head toward the herd from far up the mountain. They turned out to be a buck and a lone doe, the buck having nice horns in the 13 to 14 inch range.

"The newcomers stopped about 100 yards from the herd and stared. Then the buck shook his head. At this, the big buck in the herd leapt to his feet, stood for a moment, and then charged the intruder who ran to meet him. Just as a head-on crash seemed imminent, my hero, the big buck, made a sharp 90 degree turn and did a speedy exit stage right for some 200 yards, leaving the smaller buck surrounded by an unexpected wealth of antelope femininity.

"Unknowingly, the big buck had solved my stalking problem when he ran away, for now as he gazed back at his paradise lost, undoubtedly pondering the fickle fortunes of antelope love and war. He was less than 200 yards from the top of a low ridge which I could reach without being seen.

"Half an hour later, I belly-crawled the last few feet to the ridge crest and peered around a sagebrush. I first saw the heavy black horns, then the buck's body as he stood broadside, jealously looking back towards the invader and his spoils. As the crosshairs of the Redfield on my 6mm custom Mauser settled behind the buck's foreleg, I couldn't help but think that his luck this day had been as poor as that of the hunter who had sought him so earnestly the year before. The 85 grain Nosler sped across the 160 yards to the buck and after the short frantic dash indicative of a heart-shot animal, he was mine.

"This buck had 15 6/8" and 15 4/8" horns which were heavy all the way to the tips, enabling him to score 85 2/8 Boone and Crockett points, thus placing him a four-way tie for fifth place of all Oregon antelope taken through 1981. Since then, in 1985, two larger heads were taken in Lake County. This was the second Oregon antelope tag I'd drawn and the se-

Pronghorn antelope are wary game and are said to have vision equal to 8 power binoculars.

cond record book buck I'd taken in this unit, the first being an 83 6/8 point head taken the first year the unit was opened in 1976."

This is Eldon Buckner's story, in his own words, of how he took a trophy Boone & Crockett antelope from the sage-covered vastness of southern Oregon's Lake County in August of 1981. Buckner is a resident of Baker, Oregon, has been an official measurer for the Boone & Crockett since 1968, a range-wildlife staff officer for the U.S. Forest Service in Arizona, and one time guide for antelope hunters. He is one of Oregon's foremost authorities on antelope, having viewed, studied and measured untold numbers of antelope. His help in writing this chapter on antelope hunting in Oregon is much appreciated.

The pronghorn is one of the smallest North American big game species. Large bucks will often weigh up to 130 pounds but the average is closer to 100 pounds. Both sexes have true horns; however, the buck's are much longer and wider. Antelope are tan and buff in color with a white rump patch with hair that erects and "flashes" when danger is near.

They are built for speed with oversized heart and lungs for increased oxygen demands and their hooves have extra padding for protection from the rocky terrain. They are terrified of wire fencing and why not — hitting a barbed-wire fence at 60 mph can mean severe injury or death.

Antelope are a wary game animal whose only real natural enemies are man and coyotes. Man they can usually avoid as their vision is said to

Craig Ely with a good antelope taken in the Steens unit of southeastern Oregon. About 1,500 tags are offered each year in Oregon. (Photo courtesy Craig Ely)

equal 8 power binoculars. If hunting pressure gets too high, they will leave their favorite habitat of wide open sage flats and head for higher terrain and the security of juniper thickets. Adult pronghorn rarely fall prey to roaming coyotes. However, young antelope called kids, are extremely vulnerable to the "desert dogs" the first few days after birth.

If you like juniper trees and sagebrush, hot summer days and little hunting pressure, then Oregon antelope hunting is for you. One main problem exists — Oregon's pronghorn population is limited and competition for the 1,000 or so tags issued by the Oregon Department of Fish and Wildlife is quite high. Thousands of anxious hunters apply each year but only about 20% get lucky. Oregonians were offered 24 rifle, 3 archery, and 2 muzzleloader hunts during the 1986 hunting season. If the luck of the draw is yours, chances for success are good. Hunters average about 70% success even though the season only lasts about five days.

WHERE TO HUNT

Pronghorn are eastside species that inhabit the wide open spaces of the high desert. With the exception of the Lookout Mountain unit east of Baker, the majority of Oregon's antelope population is spread around the southeastern section of the state. Most experts agree that highest concentrations of animals and best hunting is found southeast of Burns in the

1986 ANTELOPE HARVEST

Hunt Name	Hunt Number	Tags Authorized	Tags Issued	Hunters	Hunter Days	Harvest Does	Harvest Bucks	Harvest Total	Percent Hunter Success
North Paulina	435A	15	15	14	54		3	3	21
South Paulina-North Wagontire	435B	50	50	48	184		32	32	67
Maury	436	50	50	46	166		29	29	63
Ochoco	437	110	110	103	283		70	70	68
Grizzly	438	10	10	8	13		6	6	75
Murderers Creek	446	50	50	40	124		26	26	65
North Sumpter	451A	10	10	10	28		9	9	90
South Sumpter	451B	10	10	10	20		9	9	90
Lookout Mtn.	464	15	15	12	28		12	12	100
Beulah	465	60	60	58	152		46	46	79
Malheur River	466	125	125	114	338		71	71	62
Owyhee	467	90	90	80	219		64	64	80
Whitehorse	468	135	135	133	497		69	69	52
Steens Mountain	469	126	126	119	426		54	54	45
East Beatys Butte	470A	125	125	118	375		97	97	82
West Beatys Butte	470B	125	125	121	420		76	76	63
Hart Mtn. Refuge	470C	20	20	20	64		18	18	90
Juniper	471	50	50	48	162		25	25	52
Silvies	472	75	75	72	179		55	55	76
South Wagontire	473A	60	60	58	225		22	22	38
Warner	474	90	90	78	318		42	42	54
East Interstate	475A	50	50	50	144		32	32	64
East Fort Rock-Silver Lake	476A	30	30	30	114		14	14	47
RIFLE BUCK TOTALS		1,480	1,481	1,390	4,533		881	881	63
West Fort Rock (Either Sex)	477A	50	50	46	160	6		6	13
EITHER SEX TOTALS		50	50	46	160	6		6	13
Grizzly Bow	438A	50	50	38	152		2	2	5
Gerber Reservoir Bow	475B	250	250	215	965		10	10	5
Gerber Reservoir Bow	475C	200	117	72	295		0	0	0
BOW TOTALS		500	417	325	1,412		12	12	4
Gerber Reservoir Muzzleloader	475M	20	20	20	86		6	6	30
West Fork Rock Muzzleloader	477M	50	50	49	194		0	0	0
MUZZLELOADER TOTALS		70	70	69	280		6	6	9
GRAND TOTAL 29 HUNTS		2,100	2,018	1,830	6,385		905	905	49

Courtesy Oregon Department of Fish & Game

Malheur, Owyhee, Whitehorse, Steens Mountain, and East and West Beatys units.

HOW TO HUNT

Unless you are thoroughly familiar with the unit you intend to hunt, a couple days spent scouting the area is time not wasted. Locate the animals and take the time to learn their habits and daily routines. Try to learn their routes to favorite feeding areas, where afternoon watering holes are located, and where animals bed down during the heat of the day. Good scouting will usually pay off, especially on opening day before normal daily routines are interrupted by vehicle traffic and excited hunters.

Next to an accurate and flat-shooting rifle, the most important piece of hunting equipment is a good pair of binoculars of at least 8 power — 10 power are better. Also, a 20 to 30 power spotting scope is worth its weight in gold as it will cut down on unnecessary stalks and make a legal buck or trophy identification much easier. A legal buck can be identified up to one-half mile away with the aid of a good spotting scope.

Jeeps, 4-wheel drive pickups, motorcycles and ATVs all can be used for antelope hunting. It's illegal to shoot from a motorized vehicle in Oregon, but they are very useful for getting a hunter deep into antelope country and oftentimes will put a hunter within reasonable stalking range.

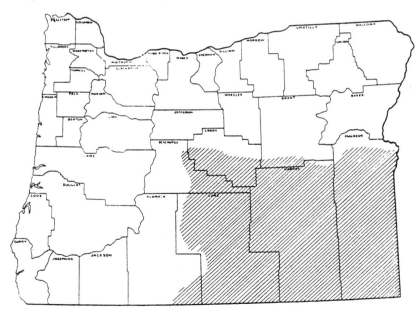

Pronghorn Antelope Range

Antelope are usually found in sagebrush flats and stalking within rifle range is often very difficult. Long shots and a flat-shooting rifle are the rule in antelope hunting. (Photo courtesy Oregon Department of Fish and Wildlife)

Stalking antelope after you locate a herd or individual is by no means easy under normal circumstances. An antelope depends on his 8 power vision more than he does his nose to alert him to possible danger. The idea is to stay completely out of sight during the entire stalk. The successful hunter takes full advantage of rolling hills, uneven terrain and small gullies to complete a successful stalk that may cover five miles or more.

TROPHY ANTELOPE

Antelope are one of the most difficult North American big game animals to size-up prior to the shot due to their small body and horn size. They are usually seen and shot at long ranges which makes trophy estimation even more difficult. Bucks characteristically carry their head in a manner that gives the impression their horns are longer than they really are. A good rule of thumb to follow is that antelope horns always measure less than they appear.

Pronghorn are taken largely for their trophy headgear even though the meat is of excellent quality when properly cared for. It is therefore important a hunter know how to judge trophy size horns. An animal with 13 inch horns is considered a good trophy and a 15 incher is a real wall-hanger. A mature pronghorn is trophy size if the horns are at least one-

Try to make a clean stalk and avoid a running shot. Antelope can reach speeds of 60 miles per hour.

third of its body length or, if looking at the animal head on or from the rear, its horn spread exceeds half its body width.

In general, Oregon antelope do not have long horns, but they have very heavy horns with long prongs. This, according to Eldon Buckner, an official measurer for Boone and Crockett, enables a fair number of Oregon antelope to meet the minimum Boone and Crockett score of 82. Even so, Oregon is still just marginal in terms of trophy animals available to the hunter. The Boone and Crockett Club ranks the top 340 trophy antelope. Oregon hunters have managed to place about 40 heads in the book, the largest being taken by E.C. Starr in 1942 at Guano Creek. It scored an amazing 90 points with horns measuring 19 4/8 and 19 5/8 inches.

Whether you go to the field to take a record buck or merely to collect a "legal" head, the hunting trip will be enjoyable. From the scouting time prior to the hunt and through the final stalk, Oregon antelope hunting is an event you'll want to repeat again and again.

Chapter 6

BLACK BEAR

The day I waited for so long had finally arrived. I was just 16 and my father promised I could use the family car for one evening. This day had been carefully planned for several years. I was going bear hunting all by myself!

I grew up hunting the many clearcuts and logging roads that surround my hometown, Seaside, Oregon. The canyon I had chosen for my first hunt seemed perfect. It had been logged five years earlier and lush green salal bushes with their plump blue berries were now about three feet high. Proof that bear were now using the area was evident by the many piles of berry-stained droppings. I knew of several hunters that had taken bear from this area and August was supposed to be the best month for bear hunting.

I parked the car about one-half mile from my selected hunting site and began a slow, cautious walk to the end of the road and an old landing. I found a large stump that provided a good view of the entire canyon. It was now 4 p.m. and I planned to sit and wait until dark — nearly four hours away.

Roughly two hours had passed when suddenly I detected some loud noises in the salal on the far hillside. I quietly chambered a round into my father's 30-06 Winchester and lay down in a prone position. After much noise and many nervous minutes, a robust black bear appeared on a large white log that jutted from the salal. I guessed the range at 350 yards and held the crosshairs just above the top of his back. The bear seemed unbothered as I squeezed off my first shot. A hint of panic swept over me as I bolted another round into the chamber. Could I have overestimated the range? I held for the bruin's shoulder and touched off my second shot. This time the big fellow tumbled off the log and disappeared into the thick green foliage. Immediately the quiet canyon erupted with the sounds of

Black bear. (Photo courtesy Oregon Department of Fish and Wildlife)

breaking brush and a series of terrifying growls. This continued for several minutes and then came an eerie silence.

I hurried down the canyon but approached the final 50 yards with extreme caution. I found the bear where it had fallen off the log. It was stone dead. It was a fine 200 pound boar with a white patch in the center of his chest. My first bear and what a thrill!

Oregon has top-notch black bear hunting, no question about it. Each year about 15,000 sportsmen purchase bear tags and take between 1,000 and 2,000 bear. The number of bear in Oregon is far greater than most people think. According to the Oregon Department of Fish and Wildlife's Black Bear Management Plan, Oregon has an estimated population of 25,000. Hunter success ranges between 5 and 50% depending on how and what part of the state you hunt. Oregonians are allowed plenty of hunting opportunity with a three month season. The season begins in mid-August and ends in late November — plenty of time to collect a nice trophy.

A bear pursuit season currently allows houndsmen an opportunity to train dogs from July 15 to no later than one week prior to the take season. The pursuit season has generated much controversy and Oregon's bear management plan calls for its elimination in favor of an earlier opening date for the general season, probably Aug. 1.

The greatest black bear ever killed in Oregon was shot by Martin Pernoll. It was killed in 1967 near Summer Lake and scored 21 10/16 Boone and Crockett points.

TROPHY BLACK BEAR

Although the Beaver State has a relatively large number of bear, Oregon is not known for trophy-size animals. The most recent copy of the Boone and Crockett record book lists only two bear taken from Oregon: Number 18 was shot in 1967 by Martin V. Pernoll in Lake County, and Number 59 was shot in 1968 by Joe W. Latimer in Curry County. The average black bear in Oregon is around 175 pounds with the boars running somewhat larger than sows. A 200 pound sow is quite large while 300 pound boars are not that uncommon.

Sizing up a trophy black bear is a difficult chore indeed. The size of the skull, adding the greatest width and length, with a minimum score of 21

Larry Dimmick with a 175-pound sow he packed out of the canyon in the background. This fall-killed bear had an unusually fine pelt and was shot with a 280 Remington in Douglas County.

inches, is used to determine ranking in the Boone and Crockett Record Club. It is, however, impractical to try and guess a bear's skull size so one must look for a large bear and hope he has a proportionately large skull.

The best way to estimate a bear's size is from a well defined track. A good rule-of-thumb is to add one inch to the measurement of a bears front pad and convert the resulting figure to feet. The result will be the size of a bear's "squared hide", that is the measurement of a hides length and width divided by two. A black bear whose hide "squares out" at six feet is a good trophy.

In general, a mature boar is larger than a mature sow. A big bear traveling alone is likely to be a boar. A very large boar is usuallly a very fat bear by mid-August. If you see a lone bear that appears large and if his hide seems to roll as he walks or runs, chances are that it is a very large boar of trophy class.

HOW TO HUNT

Each year many blackies are taken incidentally by deer or elk hunters as the opportunity presents itself. Aside from that, there are three distinct hunting methods: hunting with dogs, hunting over bait, and one-on-one stand or stalk hunting. Hound hunting is by far the most successful technique. About 10% of Oregon hunters use dogs but they account for around 40% of the total bear harvest. Their success rate is about 25% — quite high.

Hunting bear with the use of bait is legal in Oregon and becoming more popular each year. It is a most effective hunting technique. Terry Newport is a longtime hunter and very successful bear guide from the Reedsport area of southwestern Oregon. Terry hunts bear exclusively over bait while most other guides use hounds. According to Newport, "Baiting bear is the most efficient way to hunt, especially here in southwestern Oregon where we have so many." He starts baiting two to three weeks before the season in good habitat and prefers meat from a horse or beef as his bait. Hunters with weak stomachs take heed — the more rotten the meat and the stronger the smell the better it works. Baiting really works for Newport as his clients have had 100% success at getting a shot, be they rifle or archery hunters.

Stalking bear one-on-one or stand-hunting for old blackie is the least popular hunting method. It is also the only way I will hunt black bear as I feel it offers the most hunting challenge and gives the bear a sporting chance. Wayne Bergeson is a north coast resident of Clatsop County and has probably killed more bear in Oregon than any man now living. He taught me the art of hunting from a stand for black bear and has killed hundreds of bear behind dogs while working as a damage control agent for various timber companies. When I asked him which bear hunting technique he preferred, he replied, "I love to follow a pack of seasoned

Wayne Bergerson with an average bear taken in Clatsop County. Wayne is probably the best bear hunter alive in Oregon today. Through damage control and sport hunting, he has over 400 bear to his credit.

hounds as they chase a big one, but hunting bear alone and on foot is where the skill really shows." I agree.

Each year I look forward to August and the start of bear season with eager anticipation. Memories of bear hunts as a youth always seem to return. I started hunting at age 16, have now been at it for 22 years, and have taken 10 bear while stand-hunting — about a 45% success rate. I know several other hunters that use the same method with similar results.

Bears are very noisy and when still-hunting, you will usually hear the critter before you see him. Other than a rifle your best weapon is a set of good ears.

This brings to mind one memorable hunt. I had located a well used skunk cabbage patch near Eel Lake on the southern Oregon coast. Fresh tracks were everywhere and I was full of optimism. The skunk cabbage was exceptionally high, so I climbed to the top of an overturned root wad and began to wait. I was tired and promptly fell asleep, only to be awakened about 20 minutes later by some loud noises. The sound of breaking cabbage leaves and sloshing mud grew progressively louder. In fact, there was so much noise I fully expected a herd of elk to appear. To be safe, I levered a cartridge in my 358 Savage and waited. Finally, about 100 yards away, I saw the four foot high leaves parting and caught a glimpse of black hair. I could not get a clear shot until the animal finally exposed its head and neck at only 25 yards. My 250 grain silvertip found

OREGON BEAR HUNTING SEASONS & HARVEST

Year	Season Dates	Covered by Hunting Regulations		Tags Sold	Number Hunters	Bear Taken	Hunter Success	Hunter Days	Days/Hunter	Days/Bear
1975	July 01-Dec. 31/ Aug. 01-Nov. 30	Entire State		17,924	16,247	1,841	11%	148,092	9	80
1976	Aug. 01-Dec. 31/ Aug. 01-Nov. 30	Entire State		14,660	11,043	1,074	10%	102,557	9	96
1977	Aug. 01-Dec. 31/ Aug. 01-Nov. 30	Entire State		15,847	12,833	920	7%	133,570	10	145
1987	Aug. 01-Dec. 31	3/4 of State	Tag sale deadline begun	8,770*	No Survey	506	--	--	--	--
1979	Sept. 01-Nov. 30	3/4 of State		15,705*	11,324	812	7%	118,338	10	146
1980	Aug. 23-Nov. 30	Entire State		14,762*	11,072	958	9%	--	--	--
1981	Aug. 29-Nov. 30	Entire State		15,503*	10,124	783	8%	113,722	11	145
1982	Sept. 04-Nov. 30	Entire State	No tag sale deadline?	21,586*	16,756	1,313	8%	196,713	12	150
1983	Aug. 27-Nov. 30	Entire State	Tag sale deadline with deer opening	25,474*	20,500	1,420	7%	314,315	15	221
1984	Aug. 25-Nov. 30	Entire State		26,753*	No Survey	(1,350)**	--	--	--	--
1985	Aug. 24-Nov. 30	Entire State		25,863*	No Survey	(1,250)**	--	--	--	--
1986	Aug. 23-Nov. 30	Entire State		25,364*	20,297	1,347	7%	234,144	12	174

* Tag sale deadline.
** Based on report card returns.

Courtesy Oregon Department of Fish & Game

its mark and the 175 pound sow was mine. If that bear had been more quiet, I would have slept through the entire event.

My formula for successful bear hunting is not very complex. I find what they are feeding on and take time to learn their habits. I usually spend a couple of weeks driving the clearcuts and hiking in remote areas in an effort to locate prime feeding grounds. It is a good idea to have several well-used feeding areas scouted prior to opening day, which is usually in late August. Once you know where and what bear are feeding on, the hard part is over and the fun begins.

SWAMPS: One of the black bear's favorite foods in western Oregon is the skunk cabbage. Identified by its large green leaves which can reach a height of four feet and its bright yellow flowers, this plant grows only in very swampy locations. Both the juicy leaves and "corn" from the flower are eaten by bear from early spring through September. Find yourself downwind from a patch of skunk cabbage and you will quickly understand how this plant acquired its name. My son and I have taken four bear from swamps infested with this "wild cabbage" and all were killed the last week in August. Swamp bear can be hunted throughout the day. However, I prefer evening hunts starting three hours before dark.

BERRY PATCHES: Berries are no doubt a black bear's favorite food. They gorge themselves on bright, orange, salmon berries that first appear in June but are usually gone by hunting season. Blackberries are abundant throughout the summer. However, finding a large enough patch to attract returning bear is often difficult. I prefer to hunt large stands of evergreen huckleberry or dense stands of salal thickets.

Huckleberry is found in most of parts of western Oregon although reliable bear-producing stands are often difficult to find. Look for clearcuts that were logged four or five years prior and try to find huckleberry bushes at least three feet high. Find a good patch with lots of sign and wait for evening action.

Salal bushes, with their plump purple berries, also attract hungry bruins from July through September. Salal grows best on the central and northern Oregon coast but good concentrations are scattered throughout western Oregon and the Cascades.

APPLE ORCHARDS: Ask the farmers who live just about anywhere in Oregon to find bear during the months of September and October and many will quickly answer that apple orchards are the best choice. Most berries have disappeared by September when apples are just beginning to ripen—black bear have a hard time resisting the taste of juicy, ripe apples. This fruit is also a favorite food of blacktail deer and many a deer hunter has nailed a bear while waiting for a buck in his favorite orchard.

Locate a likely looking orchard and spend time looking for evidence that bear have been feeding on a regular basis. Look for tracks below the trees and the telltale droppings filled with chunks of apple. Bear don't necessarily wait for apples to drop to the ground. Examine the tree trunks

Black bear are often found throughout the summer and fall feeding on skunk cabbage plants that thrive in coastal swamps. They prefer the yellow "corn" found in the center of the plant.

The author and friend, Larry Dimmick, with two nice bear killed near Reedsport. Both bear were stalked and shot while they were feeding on huckleberries. Rifles used were a Ruger 257 Roberts and a Remington 280.

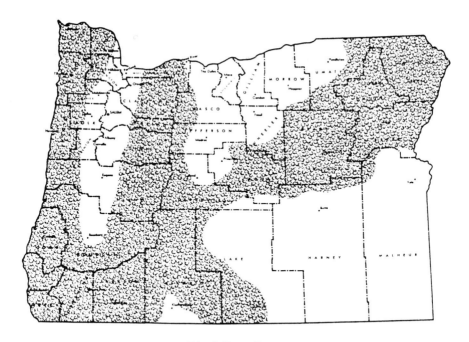

Black Bear Range

for fresh claw marks and look up high for broken branches. Should you determine regular use by one or more bear, station yourself 100 yards or so downwind and be patient.

WHERE TO HUNT

The majority of bear taken in Oregon come from west of the Cascade Mountains, especially southwestern Oregon. Southwestern Oregon has the largest bear population in the state and offers the best chance for success. According to Bill Hines, district wildlife biologist with the Oregon Department of Fish and Wildlife for southwestern Oregon, the Alsea and any coastal units south of there offer excellent opportunities for hunter success. Oregon Department of Fish and Wildlife hunting statistics show that most bear come from the Applegate, Tioga, Siuslaw and Alsea units in that order. I've hunted most of the Oregon coast and my first choice would be the Tioga unit for top notch bear hunting.

A fair number of bear come from northeastern Oregon especially the Imnaha, Chesnimnus, Snake River units. First choice for the best hunting area in the northeast would be the Snake River unit. According to Vic Coggins, Oregon Department of Fish and Wildlife's district wildlife biologist for northeastern Oregon, the Snake River unit offers great bear hunting during the special spring permit hunt and the early fall season.

This large boar was shot by the author using a 350 Remington magnum. The bear narrowly missed the record book.

Coggins states, "The Snake River unit has a very high population of black bear and for those hunters who consider the brown colored black bear an unusual trophy, that color phase represents the majority of bear in this unit. Also the Snake unit has a fair number of cinnamon colored bear — a real rarity elsewhere." In fact, biologists report that eastern Oregon black bear populations in general contain three brown to every two black color phases. Western Oregon blacks outnumber brown phases four to one.

TAKE CARE OF YOUR TROPHY

About one-half of the hunters you talk to are fond of bear meat, while the other half gag at the thought of it. I suspect those who will not eat bear have tried eating a very old and tough one or a blackie that was taken after eating dead fish or other carrion. A young berry fed bear shot during August or September makes excellent table fare. The sooner you butcher a bear the better. Bear, like pork, should be hung only a short time. And, like pork, bear meat should be well cooked to prevent trichinosis.

Salt or freeze the hide as soon as possible. Unlike deer or elk hides, a bear skin spoils quickly and the hair begins to slip. A bear skin rug or tanned bear hide makes a very impressive trophy. If the average hunter is willing to put in the necessary time and effort, he should have little trouble collecting a bear rug in Oregon.

Hunters of yesteryear with a large black bear taken in Douglas County near Elkton. (Douglas County Museum Photograph)

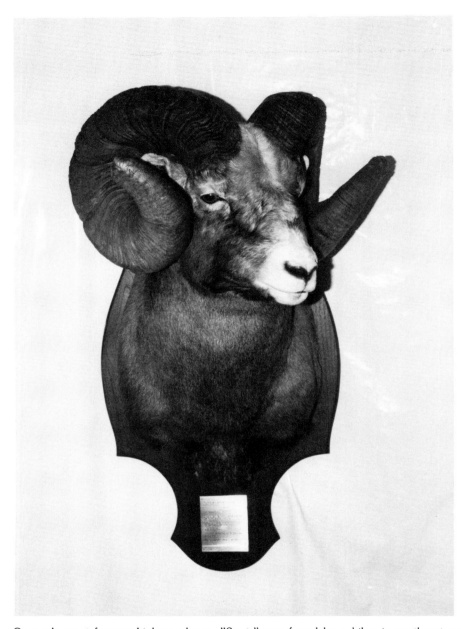

Oregon's most famous bighorn sheep, "Spot," was found by a hiker in northeastern Oregon. The massive horns scored 202 7/8 points and are listed as Number Five in the world. (Photo courtesy Weibel Taxidermy.)

Chapter 7

BIGHORN SHEEP

By now most hunters are aware of "Spot", Oregon's world class bighorn sheep found dead in the Eagle Cap Wilderness Area in 1986. Spot's horns measure an incredible 202 7/8, ranking him the Number One in the United States and Number Five in the world.

Even more impressive is the accomplishment of Portland's Nick Gianopoulos when he stalked and killed the largest bighorn any hunter has ever taken in the state of Oregon in September of 1986. The following is Nick's own account of his record-setting hunt in the Hurricane Divide area in northeastern Oregon:

"That night we got little sleep. There were storms all night and we also discovered that the roof of our cabin had a few gaps in it. Tuesday, Sept. 16 at 4 in the morning, we reluctantly crawled out of our sleeping bags, rekindled the fire and prepared breakfast. The plan was to climb up into the basin we had selected the day before, along a creek which emptied out of it, and explore as much of the top as we could. We were at the southern end of the Hurricane Divide and during the course of the next few days, we would slowly move north. We finished our meal, assembled our gear for the day and waited. A thick fog had moved in, which forced us to delay our early morning hunt. Luckily, it soon lifted enough for us to see the bottom of the creek.

"As we approached the base of the mountain, we found a well-worn game trail which headed in the direction we wanted to go. As usual the trail led us along the best, if not the only way up the hillside. The fog is still with us but gradually lifting. After 45 minutes of slow climbing, the trail finally brought us next to the creek. At that point we realized that the cliffs had forced us into the creek and that we would have to cross it to continue climbing. Steve Gianopoulos led the way as we cautiously descended into the creek bottom. Not more than two steps later Steve suddenly spun around and said, 'Nick, a sheep!' I looked across the creek and up the

The largest ram ever taken by a hunter in Oregon was shot by Nick Gianopoulos in 1986 and scored 182 4/8 points. (Photo courtesy Nick Gianopoulous.)

hillside and saw a nice ram standing broadside. Up until this moment we hadn't seen any sheep at all and even the sight of a ewe would have been gratifying. The wind was in our favor plus the sound of the creek masked our voices. The ram didn't appear overly concerned so we studied him a bit. It was a very nice ram and we figured it would score around 170 Boone and Crockett points. He certainly wasn't Spot, but I wasn't willing to risk going home empty-handed.

"Just as I had resigned to take him, I noticed another ram about 70 yards to the right of the first one. It was in the open and calmly feeding, legal but definitely smaller than the first one. I began to wonder if we were seeing all the sheep which might be on the hillside. Just then Steve said, 'I saw something move behind that tree.'

"'Is it a ram?' I asked.

"'I don't know, but it's to the right of the first one.' I looked, but was unable to see anything.

"All of a sudden another ram trotted in front of the first one. Steve exclaimed, 'Nick, it's Spot! It's Spot!'

"When I got a glimpse of its head with horns so massive that I couldn't see its eye, I thought he might be right. We could no longer see the ram from where we were so I took a few steps down the hill until he was in sight again. He was now standing broadside to me in front of the first ram and looking right at me. I studied him through the scope and knew right

Bighorn sheep. (Photo courtesy Oregon Department of Fish and Wildlife)

away he wasn't Spot and that he would not remain in the opening all day. The smaller ram moved off to the left and Steve could not see the big ram from where he was. He could only watch me as I took aim and fired my 25-06. To our horror, the ram I shot bounded up the hill with the other ram close behind. The lead ram took only two jumps then collapsed and tumbled a few yards. When we got to it, a close-up look of those huge horns and body overwhelmed us. It was obvious we had something special. The horns measured 15 inches around the base and 40 1/2 inches long — a new state record measuring 188 3/8 Boone and Crockett points."

Bighorn sheep were once native to most of eastern Oregon. The Rocky Mountain subspecies inhabited the northeastern section of the state. The California subspecies resided over much of southeastern Oregon and through much of the John Day and Deschutes River drainages.

Indiscriminate hunting and overgrazing by domestic livestock and their accompanying diseases led to the eventual demise of Oregon's native bighorns. The last California bighorn disappeared from southeastern Oregon about 1915. The last Rocky Mountain bighorn were gone from northeastern Oregon by 1945.

In November 1954, 20 California bighorn sheep were trapped near Williams Lake, British Columbia, and released in a holding pasture on the west face of Hart Mountain in southeastern Oregon. Nearly 200 California bighorn have since been trapped on Hart Mountain and transplanted to 10 Oregon sites.

Rocky Mountain bighorn were reintroduced to northeastern Oregon in 1971. Twenty animals from Jasper Park, Alberta were released in Hells Canyon but eventually disappeared. An additional 20 Jasper Park bighorns were released in the Silver Creek burn on the Lostine River in November of 1971. This population has flourished and has been Oregon's source of Rocky Mountain transplant stock. These transplants have resulted in re-establishment of populations of Rocky Mountain and California bighorn back to their native range. Oregon hunters can thank the Oregon Department of Fish and Wildlife for present and future bighorn sheep hunting opportunities in Oregon.

According to the Oregon Department of Fish and Wildlife's Bighorn Sheep Management Plan, the estimated summer population of the 11 California bighorn herds in Oregon was 1,250 animals in 1986. The four Rocky Mountain bighorn herds in northeastern Oregon were estimated at 290 head.

Hunting opportunities for bighorn sheep in Oregon are still fairly limited with 50 tags or less offered annually: 44 in 1987 and 42 in 1988. The majority (80 to 90%) of sheep tags offered are for the California bighorn. Chances for success in drawing are low, ranging from .5 to 1.5%. In 1987 the Oregon Legislature passed a law requiring that 5 to 10% of the tags be offered to nonresidents. A legal ram is one that has a 3/4 curl or better and a hunter may obtain only one bighorn sheep tag in a lifetime. For those hunters who draw a sheep tag, success rate is high averaging about 75%.

Since 1987, one Oregon sheep tag has been auctioned to the highest bidder which is allowed by the Oregon legislature and sanctioned by the Oregon Department of Fish and Wildlife. The minimum bid in 1987 was $20,000 and the final high bid was $56,000. All funds raised are earmarked specifically for wild sheep management in Oregon.

HOW TO HUNT

Good physical conditioning is extremely important when making a sheep hunt. Sheep, like Rocky Mountain goats, avoid natural enemies and predation by inhabiting steep and rugged terrain. You will not find roads and 4-wheel drives, and ATV are useless to the sheep hunter. It's all leg and lung power and the better your physical condition, the better your chances for a successful hunt.

Pre-hunt scouting will increase the odds for success. In Oregon, every hunter is required to attend a sheep hunting seminar before the actual hunting season begins. Here the Oregon Department of Fish and Wildlife biologists and other experts tell hunters which size animals can be taken, approximately where the animals are located and give other helpful hun-

BIGHORN SHEEP POPULATION & COMPOSITION STATUS

PER 100 EWES

Area	Population Estimate		Lambs			Rams			Number Rams Observ	
			1986	1985	1984	1986	1985	1984	Total	3/4 Curl+
CALIFORNIA BIGHORN										
Hart Mtn.	450	(306)	38	-	49	60	-	50	87	59
Juniper-Warner	50	(-)	-	22	-	-	22	100	-	-
Aldrich Mtns.	80	(43)	61	50	-	78	90	-	14	4
Steens	275	(168)	35	14	33	25	44	47	26	17
Pueblo-(Alvord)	100	(53)	36	40	29	54	13	19	15	8
Owyhee	225	(-)	-	9	43	-	52	38	-	-
ROCKY MTN. BIGHORN										
Hurricane Div.	125	(87)	33	33	54	57	35	52	26	15
Lower Imnaha*	100	(57)	-	77	45	-	42	69	11	5

*June Counts

Courtesy Oregon Department of Fish & Game

The largest California bighorn sheep from Oregon was shot by John Sherman in 1983 in the Steens Mountains. It scored 175 4/8. (Photo courtesy John Sherman)

ting hints. Before the actual hunt, spend at least two days scouting the area and learning the habits of the animals you will be hunting.

Oregon sheep season runs from late August through early October and weather conditions can vary dramatically at these higher elevations. Bring proper clothing and be prepared for severe weather changes from 90 degree heat to a howling blizzard. My experience has been that layers of light clothing work best as you hike and sweat in steep country. It seems like you are constantly putting on or taking off shirts and jackets.

Take a good **comfortable** backpack with everything you need to spend a night on the mountain if necessary. I once got caught in a raging snowstorm high atop Alaska's Wrangell Mountains without such provi-

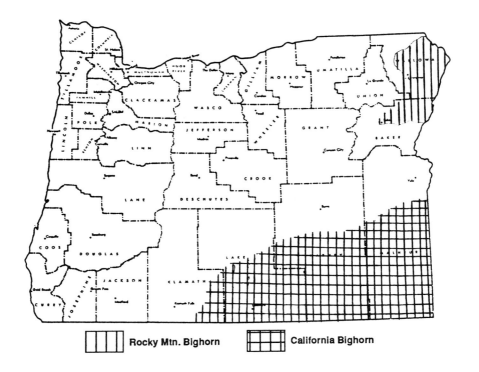

Rocky Mtn. Bighorn   California Bighorn

Bighorn Sheep Range

sions. The day began with clear blue skies and three hours later my brother and I were struggling on numb legs down treacherous snow-covered slopes trying to make our spike camp far below. Luckily we made the camp with our lives intact. Had we been prepared with emergency shelter and warmth, we could have weathered that freak fall storm and not been forced to risk our lives in desperate need to reach our camp. Oregon fall weather can be just as deadly.

This section would not be complete without some mention of the proper weapon for mountain hunting. Any caliber from 243 on up is adequate for sheep providing bullet construction is good and the weapon is properly sighted-in. Light rifles with relatively short barrels are the rule in sheep or goat hunting. A lightweight rifle is a blessing on steep terrain with a heavy pack and a short barrel may save your life when a rock outcropping is dangerously close as you work your way around a cliff for a better shot. A good scope and sling are the final accessories that round-out a good mountain rifle.

A good California bighorn taken by Don Letts on the east face of the Steens Mountains. (Photo courtesy Don Letts)

TROPHY SHEEP

Until recently, bighorn sheep have not inhabited Oregon in huntable numbers and therefore only a few have made the Boone and Crockett Club. All four rams to meet the minimum score of 180 points were the Rocky Mountain variety and came from northeastern Oregon. "Spot's" horns were found by a hiker, measured 202 7/8 points, and are listed as Number Five in the world. As mentioned earlier, the largest ram ever taken in Oregon by a hunter was shot by Nick Gianopoulos in 1986 and scored 188 3/8 points. In 1981, Randy Craddock killed a ram in Wallowa County that scored 182 4/8 points. Kirt Jones collected a bighorn trophy that went 180 3/8 points in 1979.

The California bighorn sheep of southeastern Oregon genetically have somewhat smaller horns and none from Oregon have made the Boone and Crockett's minimum entry level. At this writing, Portland's John Sherman has the largest California bighorn ever to come from Oregon. It was taken in the Steens Mountains in 1983 and measured 175 4/8 points (green measurement). In 1982, Phil Obrish shot a ram in the Steens Mountains that went 175 points (green measurement).

Field identification of trophy sheep can be tricky business. I have never been lucky enough to draw an Oregon sheep tag. However, I have hunted Dall sheep in Alaska's Wrangell Mountains. Several points are worth remembering. Good optics are an essential part of proper trophy judgement. Good quality 7 to 10 power binoculars and a spotting scope of at least 20 power (a 30 power is better) are necessary tools for sheep hunting. On my first sheep hunt to Alaska, I took 7 power glasses and a 20 power spotting scope, both of which were low quality. The spotting scope never had the power for good horn size identification and the image was always fuzzy. We came home with one full-curl between two of us and had to pass up several other rams because we were unsure of their horn size.

A hunter should be prepared to take the necessary time to judge a ram before he pulls the trigger. Never judge a ram when he is facing away. Most mature rams will look much bigger than they really are when viewed from behind. To be sure, a full head-on view is best. A sheep must have good horn weight to be of trophy class. For bighorn sheep, broomed horns usually mean the lambing points are gone and they will obviously carry more weight. A good broadside view is vital if you are looking for a trophy-class animal. To make the records book, a bighorn has to have a full curl and the bottom of the curl approximates the rear base of the lower jawbone. If after thorough examination you still have doubts whether the ram is of record class, do not shoot.

A good broadside view such as this is vital for proper trophy judgement. (Photo courtesy Oregon Department of Fish and Wildlife)

Mountain lions are making a dramatic come back in Oregon. (Photo courtesy Oregon Department of Fish and Wildlife)

Chapter 8

COUGAR

"I had seen the big cougar track for the last three years, but had not been able to find one fresh enough that the dogs could follow. The weather had warmed up and it rained hard during the night. I needed a load of grain from town which was about 24 miles away. I had to drive through some good cougar country to get there so I decided to take my four hounds and a cowdog.

"Near Cathrine Creek I stopped to look at a track that was crossing the road and heading up through some rimrocks. It was that same cat with a huge track about seven inches across and it looked to be about three days old. I turned the dogs out and they opened and took off while I was getting my.22 pistol and a candy bar. By the time I got to the top of the rim about 8:00 a.m. I could barely hear the dogs about two miles away. They headed into three foot deep snow and the going got rough since I had no snowshoes. I came to a deer kill in the head of Little Cathrine Creek that looked to be a couple of days old.

"It was now about 3:00 p.m., the snow was up to my hips, and my candy bar was long gone. The cat headed away from the kill and down a steep mountain for lower country. At about 4:00 p.m. I met the dogs coming back. I turned them around and they followed tracks to the bottom where they treed up under some large rocks. It was a mass of tracks and the dogs were treed solid.

"I was nearly at the end of my rope — all my strength and energy were nearly gone. Somehow I got to the top of the rocks where the dogs were calling. I noticed my old redbone female had separated from the rest and was treed on a bushy red fir. Finally, after several minutes, I could see the big cat partially hidden near the top. The first shot with my pistol was not solid and the cat ran around the mountain with all the dogs giving chase. It treed again and this time my shot was true.

Jason Campbell with a cougar taken near Oakridge. Dogs are a necessity if a hunter expects any chance of success while cougar hunting.

"I weighed the cat next day on certified scales. Total weight was 184 pounds and it measured 8 feet 10 inches nose to tip of tail. The green skull measurement was 15 12/16 which tied the world record then held by Teddy Roosevelt. After drying, Boone and Crockett scored it 15 10/16 which was good enough for Number 4 in the world and is still the Oregon record."

This is Ron Lay's story of how he tracked and killed the largest cougar the state has ever known. Not mentioned was the fact that Ron trailed the cat for 12 miles in snow and packed that cougar over his back for over five miles back to his pickup. A trophy well earned!

The cougar or mountain lion was considered a dastardly villain and predator supreme by Oregonians since the early days of the first territorial government. Well over 100 years would pass before conservation measures were taken to protect this monarch of the Oregon wild. The cougar was declared a game animal in 1967.

Thanks to the fact that the Oregon Game Commission declared the cougar a game animal and because of proper management by the present Oregon Department of Fish and Wildlife, mountain lions are making a dramatic comeback and there is again limited hunting opportunity. Oregon Department of Fish and Wildlife has recently completed the Cougar Management Plan that will help insure this continued increase in cougar numbers.

The Mountain Lion is a large animal with males averaging from 140 to

COUGAR HARVEST SUMMARY REPORT CARD DATA

Year	EASTERN OREGON			WESTERN OREGON			STATE TOTAL			
	Tags Authorized	Hunters	Harvest	Tags Authorized	Hunters	Harvest	Tags Authorized	Hunters	Harvest	Percent Success
1970	25	16	10				25	16	10	56
1971			15			3	100	68	18	26
1972	75	46	22				75	46	22	48
1973	83	55	16				83	55	16	29
1974	75	34	16				75	34	16	47
1975	95	52	15				95	52	15	29
1976	115	52	14	10	8	2	125	60	16	27
1977	115	54	25	25	19	2	140	73	27	37
1978	105	65	24	25	16	10	130	81	34	42
1979	115	54	19	25	17	4	140	71	23	32
1980	120	56	17	40	33	15	160	89	32	36
1981	98	52	25	43	31	8	141	83	33	38
1982	117	69	43	46	29	14	163	98	57	58
1983	132	51	41	56	34	13	188	85	54	64
1984*	167	-	42	96	-	37	263	-	79	-
1985*	207	-	36	155	-	26	362	-	62	-
1986*	232	-	62	230	-	70	462	-	132	-

*No Hunter Survey Taken

Courtesy Oregon Department of Fish & Game

The state record cougar was taken by Ron Lay near Catherine Creek in northeastern Oregon in 1966. The skull scored 15 10/16, the animal weighed 184 pounds, and it currently ranks 11th in the world. (Photo by Ron Lay)

200 pounds and measuring up to seven feet or over in length. They need all the size they can attain since all three species of deer are their main food source. An adult cougar will kill an average of one deer or more a week. The big cats stalk to within a short distance, spring upon a deer's withers and bite into the neck at the base of the skull.

HOW TO HUNT

The only consistent method for success in cougar hunting is the use of a pack of well-trained hounds, 90% of Oregon's cougar hunters use dogs. Good breeds for cougar dogs are black-and-tans, Walker, Platt, Redbone, and Blue-Tick hounds. Good lion dogs are rare indeed. On the average, only one out of 200 dogs will turn out to be exceptional.

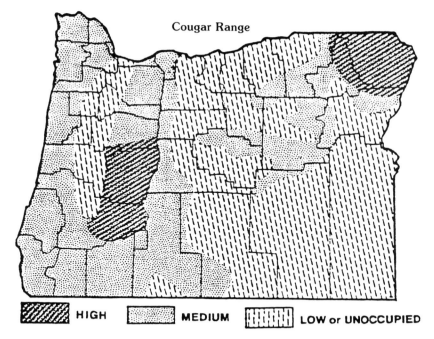

Cougar Range

HIGH ░ MEDIUM ▓ LOW or UNOCCUPIED

A good cougar hunter looks for three things other than fresh tracks: high trails, high passes between drainages, and scratchings in the ground. Only adult males scratch and the scratchings consists of dirt and needles pulled in the opposite direction the animal is traveling.

Following a pack of hounds after cougar on foot or horseback is tough business. No telling how many miles you'll travel, what the weather conditions will be or if you'll even catch up to the cat. The thrill of the hunt is in the chase in this particular sport. Once a cougar bounces out in front of the dogs the hunt is nearly over as the cat will usually run only a quarter mile or so before treeing.

A cougar that has treed will usually stay put until hunters approach. Weapons used to dispatch mountain lions range from .22 rifles and pistols to 30/30 carbines — probably the best choice. Treed cats can be shot with bow and arrow but most hound owners discourage this practice because a wounded cougar can easily kill a valuable dog. According to Oregon Department of Fish and Wildlife, there have been no documented cougar attacks on humans in Oregon. However a hunter should approach a treed cat with extreme caution.

WHERE TO HUNT

Cougar are distributed throughout Oregon and use a variety of habitat types that range from alpine to desert environments. Good deer country is good lion country as long as few humans inhabit the area.

Cougar hunting the way it was in Douglas County in 1915. Note the trap on the animal's leg. (Douglas County Museum Photograph)

In 1986 the Oregon Department of Fish and Wildlife issued 230 cougar tags for western Oregon. They were issued in the central coast, south coast, Santiam, McKenzie and South Cascades units. A total of 70 cats were taken and the majority (54) came from the south Cascades area. Eastern Oregon cougar hunters were issued 232 tags in 1986 and 62 cougar were harvested. All but two were taken in the extreme northeastern section of the state in the Wenaha-Snake and Wallowa's areas. Throughout the state, demand for cougar tags is high and applicants have only a 10 to 20% chance of drawing one.

Chapter 9

UPLAND BIRDS

PHEASANT

We were actually hunting chukar along some rimrocks adjacent to rolling wheat fields near Condon, Oregon, when my son shot his first pheasant. We had covered many miles with only moderate success — a half dozen chukar between us. Six roosters jumped beyond gun range, set their wings, and drifted across the golden slopes to a small patch of thistle and willows a quarter mile or so away.

Eric had never shot a pheasant and was ready to sprint the entire distance to get a shot. "Let's run, dad, before they get away," he said. I explained that they probably weren't going anywhere and that we would no doubt get some shooting since that was the only good cover for miles around.

I put Eric on the edge and I went in the center of the thicket that was only 25 yards across and about 50 yards long. We had nearly reached the end when I heard Eric say, "Think they're still here?" I was trying to explain how pheasants can hold tight even with little cover when the brush erupted and birds flushed in all directions. I've never seen anything like it before or since. There were at least two dozen birds in that patch — far more than the five or six we expected. The amazing part is that they were all roosters; I didn't see one hen. I scratched one bird down and watched Eric make a clean double. When the dust settled, Eric was one happy boy — another magic moment shared by father and son.

The ring-necked pheasant is Oregon's premiere upland game bird — hands down. Oregon Department of Fish and Wildlife hunting records show that the annual harvest had varied between 167,000 and 477,000 and between 50,000 and 100,000 hunters annually pursue this multi-colored import from the Orient.

These three early season roosters were downed with a 410 bore when the shooting was close. Best late season pheasant medicine is a full-choked 12 gauge.

Over 100 years ago Judge Owen Denny, consul-general to Shanghai, had no idea of the impact he would have on Oregon's bird hunting future as well as the rest of the nation. In 1882 he crated 70 ring-necks and sent them to his brother in Linn County who released them on his ranch near Peterson Butte, Oregon.

That Willamette Valley release proved to be the world's most outstanding transplant of a foreign game bird. Pheasant numbers increased so rapidly that by 1891 Oregon held its first pheasant hunt and had sent many birds to other states for brood stock.

The love affair between thousands of Oregon sportsmen and the ring-necked pheasant is easy to understand. Although ring-necks can be hunted on horribly steep terrain and in brush so thick it could hide a herd of elk, pheasants are generally a flatland species that are relatively easy to hunt. The thunderous rise of a big rooster will rush a surge of excitement through the veins of the most time-tested veteran. If you survive the shock of his explosive take-off, the ring-neck is a fairly easy target. The hunter is often on flat ground, a pheasant usually flies in a straight line, and his large size makes frequent hits common for a good shooter.

A mature rooster is a sight to behold. A three to four pound cock is not only a meal fit for a king, but he seems to possess every color on the rainbow. Do not, however, be fooled by his elegant colors — he is a master of camouflage. I've seen a half dozen pheasants disappear before my eyes in an open field with grass no higher than two inches. Also, if given the opportunity a pheasant would rather run than fly so a good dog is a must for consistent success.

WHERE TO HUNT

The Willamette Valley was THE place to hunt pheasants in years past. Increased hunting pressure and elimination of key habitat have reduced hunting opportunity and success drastically. The Oregon Department of Fish and Wildlife has reared and released about 20,000 game-farm pheasants annually and many were released at various locations throughout the Willamette Valley to increase hunting opportunity. Fair numbers of wild birds are found throughout the valley area. However, Lane, Linn and Marion counties are the best choices for good hunting according to Oregon Department of Fish and Wildlife harvest figures.

East of the Cascades is where to look for Oregon pheasant hunting at its best. Southeastern Oregon, especially Malheur County, consistently yields more roosters than any part of the state. The corn and sugar beet fields around the little town of Vale are inundated with anxious hunters at the start of pheasant season — usually the second or third weekend in October. The grainfields of Harney County are another fine prospect.

The rolling wheatfields of Umatilla County near Pendleton are my first choice for opening weekend. Hunting pressure seems far less than around Vale and access to private property is easier to achieve. Baker County, bordering the Snake River, is also a good bet. The Powder River near Richland and fields around Durkee on the Burnt River rear good pheasant numbers.

The fencerows and creek bottoms of Wasco and Gillian counties of northcentral Oregon have provided good pheasant hunting for years. I am especially fond of the rolling hills around Condon in the heart of Oregon wheat country.

HUNTING ACCESS

Finding access to the birds if far more difficult than the actual hunt for most Oregonians. Pheasants like agricultural land, ditches, and fencerows. Unfortunately that usually means private property.

Pheasant hunting in Oregon seems to become more and more popular with each passing year. The lucky hunters are those who are personal friends or relative of farmers or ranchers in prime pheasant country. To these chosen few, planning next seasons pheasant hunt is as simple as p.cking up the phone or sending a letter. For other hunters, like myself, each season offers the challenge of trying to find a good place to hunt.

I usually have little or no problem securing permission to try for pheasants on private property. My approach is simple. I never trespass and always go directly to the landowner's house. I try to make a good first impression and never go to the door with a beer in hand. I assure the rancher that I am a safe hunter, will not litter, and will respect his property and close all gates. This approach usually works but if he still seems reluc-

Although pheasants are normally found on fairly flat ground and are not a difficult target, they are a large bird that can absorb a lot of lead.

tant, I often offer to pay $5.00 to $10.00 for the right to hunt his property. That's a small price to pay for a chance to hunt Oregon's premiere game bird.

SEASON

Pheasant season generally opens the second weekend in October and often stays open until November unless bird numbers are quite low.

QUAIL

"How did you two do on chukar today?" asked a well-dressed rancher ·who was sitting on the other side of the restaurant.

"Not well at all," I replied. "Two weeks ago we really got the birds, but these recent rains have scattered the chukar so I guess we'll be heading home tomorrow."

As we drank coffee in that Burns, Oregon, restaurant, there was no hiding our disappointment. We had traveled several hundred miles and hunted all day. Our efforts had provided us with only two birds.

We were trying to decide how early to leave for home when the rancher asked, "You boys like to shoot quail? I must have 500 birds on my ranch and you're welcome to hunt."

He didn't have to ask twice and arrangements were made for a hunt the following morning.

The quail hunt that we enjoyed that next day was an experience I'll always remember. Each brush patch, irrigation ditch, and fencerow held a covey whose explosive flush tested our nerves and shooting ability. Hitting those six ounce speedsters was a real challenge with our tightly choked 20 gauges. By mid-afternoon, we had each shot well over a box of shells to finally fill our 10 bird limits. The nine hour trip home was filled with enthusiastic chatter about our next quail hunt.

Valley quail were originally found only in southern Oregon but today this adaptable little gamebird has flourished throughout the state — especially in eastern Oregon. Though not usually a primary species, Oregon hunters annually harvest from 100,000 to 300,000 of these feathered rockets depending on population levels.

Like other upland species in Oregon, valley quail populations can fluctuate drastically from year to year. A mild winter in the eastern section of the state will assure adequate breeding stock. If the following spring is relatively dry and nesting conditions are good, Oregon hunters can experience quail hunting at its best.

Until a few seasons ago, my upland targets were limited to chukar, pheasants and an occasional Hungarian partridge. I now enjoy quail hunting so much that I make several trips each season from my coastal home to the east side of the Cascade Mountains specifically to hunt quail. I've

Close friend and hunting buddy, Larry Dimmick, with some valley quail he shot near Fossil in central Oregon. He was using an Ithaca/SKB 20 gauge bore improved cylinder and modified.

also done some horse trading to acquire a 20 gauge double specifically for use on quail.

You could ask why I spend so much time, effort, and money to hunt a bird that has a total body weight of less than one leg of a mature pheasant. I don't consider myself a "meat hunter" when it comes to upland bird hunting. When I take to the field with my favorite shotgun, I hope to find plenty of exercise, a bird that will challenge my shooting skills, and most important, I want to burn a lot of powder. Valley quail hunting definitely fulfills all these needs.

The Oregon Fish and Wildlife hunting statistics indicate the annual harvest of pheasants is nearly twice that of valley quail and yet the overall quail population greatly exceeds that of pheasants. This lack of hunting pressure and liberal bag limits make Oregon quail hunting a most enjoyable sport. With the high mortality rate of 30 to 60% annually, Oregon Department of Fish and Wildlife management is geared to harvesting the surplus quail each year — bag limits are usually 8 to 10 birds per day.

WHERE TO HUNT

Although huntable populations of mountain quail exist in the Coast and Cascade Mountains and bobwhite quail have been introduced, valley quail are the species most Oregon hunters are after. The premier quail

My wife, Shirley, hunting quail near Durkee not far from a barn and farm house. Quail are what I call "people birds" and often hang close to barn yards, hay stacks and corrals.

hunting is in the arid regions of central and eastern Oregon. Quail harvest figures from the Oregon Department of Fish and Wildlife indicate that Malheur County is No. 1 in valley quail taken, while Umatilla County has the No. 2 slot. Following in order are Baker, Wasco, and Jefferson counties. Most of my good hunting has been confined to Malheur, Baker, and Wasco counties.

Valley quail occasionally inhabit the higher elevations. The best hunting, however, will be in low valley creek bottoms where small farms or ranch houses are likely to be situated. Quail are what I call "people birds" and, unless harassed, they tend to hang around barns, corrals, haystacks, and other man-made structures. In my wanderings, I've found that a high percentage of these lowland ranches have a flock or two of resident quail that seldom get hunted. If you notice a likely ranch that has potential for quail shooting, stop by and try to get permission to hunt. About 50% of the time you will be successful and the landowner often will point out where you are likely to find birds.

In some years, rough winters and poor nesting conditions can make chukar and pheasants hard to find. No matter how bleak the upland forecast has been, a bird hunter can always locate good numbers of quail to hunt. Each time you wander east of the Cascades to hunt quail make sure to have plenty of ammunition. Valley quail flush at speeds up to 54 mph!

HUNTING SEASON

Quail season traditionally begins the third weekend in October and will continue through November unless preseason counts are low.

The chukar is popular in Oregon.

(Photo courtesy Oregon Department of Fish and Wildlife)

Friend and hunting partner, Randy Egelhoff, with a brace of chukar in typical chukar habitat — steep and rocky. He was hunting the Burnt River and shoots a model 12 Winchester in 20 gauge.

CHUKAR

We left the Oregon Coast at midnight and fully expected to be hunting chukar along the Burnt River, near Baker, by mid-morning. Packed snow and ice slowed our journey considerably. With only five hours of daylight remaining, we started up the snow-covered canyon that seemed almost too steep to hunt. There was no sign or sound of chukar as we puffed our way up the parallel ridges. Depression set in as we reached the top an hour or so later.

"Long trip for nothing," my partner said and sighed.

"Maybe we can find some quail down low," I replied. At that moment the frozen cheatgrass seemed to explode with at least 25 chukars. How we managed to knock down two birds, I'll never know. Our lungs and legs felt totally spent, but by day's end, our game bags were heavy with limits of chukar.

For many Oregon shotgunners the chukar is **THE** bird. Chukar are native of dry southeastern Europe and parts of Asia. Attempts to establish this bird in Oregon took place over a period of years beginning in the 1930's, but it was not until the early 1950's that the species firmly took hold after a release along the John Day River near Condon. Since then, population levels rise and fall, but the relative abundance has remained high.

A chukar hunter in rather gentle terrain. Greatest concentrations are generally found in habitat somewhat steeper and with more rock outcroppings. (Photo courtesy Oregon Department of Fish and Wildlife)

Chukar hunting is not as popular in Oregon as pheasant hunting but a solid corps of hunters pursue these birds each year. Chukar hunting is, to say the least, a physically demanding sport. Depending on weather conditions and hatching success, Oregon hunters take from 100,000 to 500,000 of these "cliff climbers" each year.

I have often asked myself, if I had to choose only one gamebird to hunt, what would it be? Each time I ask this hypothetical question the answer is always the same — chukar, Oregon's finest gamebird.

I have spent 14 seasons and made more than 60 trips to hunt "gray ghosts" over peaked crags and jagged rimrocks throughout central and eastern Oregon. Friends question my fanaticism. My answer is simple. I believe chukar are the most challenging gamebird of all. It inhabits steep rocky terrain which demands that hunters be in good physical condition and possess the ability to shoot well on uneven slopes. The seasons are usually long, the limits liberal, and chukar are fine tablefare.

WHERE TO HUNT

Wherever you choose to hunt, locating birds can be a problem. Three main ingredients are necessary for good chukar habitat: steep slopes covered with cheatgrass for food, rocky outcroppings for shelter from predators and, of course, water. Find all three and you will find birds.

Flocks are relatively easy to find before the first rains. They usually come to water in the early morning and then again at mid-afternoon. Chukar make a lot of noise and their characteristic calls of "chuker-chuker-chuker" help a hunter pinpoint their location. I hunt along the creek bottoms and adjacent slopes looking for sign and listening for their distinctive chatter.

Chukar become more difficult to find after that first rain. They no longer need to travel to water and can be widely scattered. Hunt up and down ridges until you find birds or see sign, then stay at that same general elevation for best luck. A good bird dog is useful, especially for retrieving cripples, but not mandatory. When you locate a flock, always try to get above them as they usually run uphill when alarmed. Also, keep your eye on where birds land after they flush — a quick follow-up will often bring good results.

Chukar are found only on the east side of the Cascade Range. In central Oregon, the Deschutes and John Day Rivers provide prime chukar hunting. Wasco, Sherman and Deschutes counties respectively offer the best chance for success.

Two of my favorite hunting areas are along the John Day River near Condon and the rimrocks along the Deschutes River near the town of Maupin.

In the northeast part of Oregon, Baker, Gilliam, and Wheeler Counties, in that order, are traditionally the best chukar producers. Hunt in Baker County and you'll likely do well along the Burnt and Powder Rivers. The breaks of the Snake River is nationally known for its fine chukar hunting.

If you like isolation, desert air and fine chukar hunting, head to Malheur and Harney counties in southeastern Oregon. The Malheur River, between Juntura and Riverside, is one of the best areas in the state.

The area round Owyhee River and Reservoir are excellent chukar hunting prospects. However, much of the area and birds are off the beaten path and often inaccessible.

Shotgun types and gauges are a matter of personnel preference. A light pump or automatic with full or modified choke would be a good choice. A flock of these marvelous game birds are often hard to come by and that third shot can make the difference between success and failure.

HUNTING SEASON

If chukar numbers are high, the season generally opens in early October and ends in mid-January. When preseason counts are low, the season generally starts the second or third weekend in October. Limits range from 5 to 8 birds per day.

Oregon grouse hunting is gaining in popularity and 30,000 to 100,000 birds are taken annually. A short-barreled, double bored improved cylinder and modified is an excellent choice for grouse hunting. (Photo courtesy Oregon Department of Fish and Wildlife)

FOREST GROUSE

Every boy becomes a man in the eyes of his father at some point. I became a man some 30 years ago while hunting grouse along the Lewis and Clark River in Clatsop county.

Grouse hunting in northern Oregon could never be described as great. My dad, however, had flushed several ruffed grouse from an old abandoned apple orchard while he and Mom were picking apples. He thought we should give it a try. I had potted several grouse with my 410 single shot as we hunted logging roads, but never had a shot at a flying bird.

We had to walk about a half mile along an old road that had grown up in 30-year-old alders. We both had our shotguns ready because dad said that grouse like old roads along a river or creek. We came to the orchard and I was ready. Just as dad had predicted, a big grouse flushed with the roar of wings from out of a tree but we couldn't get a shot. We continued the hunt but could find no more birds. Father said our hunt was over and we started home along the edge of an open field. We were nearly to the old road when a grouse jumped from behind me and headed for the trees. The little 410 popped and down came the bird. My dad went wild with excitement. "That was the best shot I've ever seen. No grown man could have done better." And so, at the age of 11, a freckle-faced boy became a man in the eyes of his father.

Grouse hunting, especially ruffed grouse hunting is as traditional and American as apple pie. Talk with any hunter from "back East" about grouse or partridge hunting and watch him come alive with excitement. He'll tell you about the lightning flush of a ruffed grouse and the split-second reactions of a grouse hunter. He'll talk about alder and maple thickets and fine grouse guns. For many eastern sportsmen, the only sport is grouse hunting.

Grouse are far less popular here in Oregon. However, good numbers of both blue and ruffed grouse are available throughout the state. Each year Oregon hunters harvest anywhere from 30,000 to 100,000 blue and ruffed grouse from all regions of the state.

WHERE TO HUNT

In general, blue grouse are about a third larger than ruffed grouse and prefer somewhat higher altitudes. Most grouse taken in Oregon are shot by big game hunters along the roads as they hunt for deer or elk. Grouse can be taken only by shotgun in Oregon and experienced hunters always have a shotgun handy. Potting grouse while driving along a gravel road is not my idea of sport. I prefer to hunt the alder flats and creek bottoms when I am after a ruffed grouse or hunt the higher meadows and isolated timber patches when I want a big blue grouse or two.

Both blue and ruffed grouse are, in a general sense, distributed evenly

Although most grouse are taken incidentally by deer or elk hunters who carry shotguns in their rigs, alder flats, old apple orchards, and creek bottoms provide plenty of action for those willing to put forth the effort.

throughout the state with the exception of the southeastern corner of Oregon. Grouse like hills, creek bottoms, and cover — something the deserts of southeastern Oregon have very little of. If I had to pick one county in Oregon for good ruffed grouse hunting, my choice would be Clatsop county in the northwest portion of the state. For fine blue grouse hunting, it would have to be Umatilla County around Pilot Rock and Ukiah.

This chapter wouldn't be complete without a unit on guns for grouse. Most shots on grouse are close in thick cover. A fast-handling, short-barreled shotgun is the ticket. A 20 gauge, double barrel, bored, improved cylinder and modified using No. 7 1/2 or No. 8 shot is just about ideal.

SEASON

Grouse season generally begins in late August and continues through December. As mentioned earlier, most grouse are taken during deer and elk season by game hunters who carry a shotgun in their vehicle. For those who don't mind walking down an abandoned logging road, through an apple orchard or alder flat, Oregon grouse hunting is fine sport.

Male sage grouse are similar to turkeys in that they strut and display in an effort to win the favor of their selected mate. (Photo courtesy Oregon Department of Fish and Wildlife)

SAGE GROUSE

Few experiences can match the thrill of a dozen sage grouse flushing, one after another, out of knee-high sagebrush. It takes steady nerves to remain calm and shoot accurately during such a spectacle. These large five to six pound birds provide sporty shooting, and you don't need guides, dogs, or specialized equipment.

"Sage Hens" are atypical game birds that live on open, semi-arid plains and foothills. They are uniquely adapted to this environment, feeding on sagebrush and seasonal green plants. They are usually found in flocks and close to water during summer and early fall. Sage grouse are found throughout various locations in eastern Oregon. However, Malheur County has one of the best populations.

Finding birds in the seemingly endless expanses of sagebrush can be frustrating. Hunting season usually falls in September and sage hens tend to concentrate near dependable water sources in areas with green feed. The most productive hunting method is the organized drive with between 2 and 20 hunters.

Sage grouse can be difficult to bring down because they are large, powerful birds. A full-choked, 12 gauge with No.4 shot is best.

Up to 20,000 sage grouse were taken annually during the early 50's. However, populations have declined and hunting opportunities have been limited during recent years. Hunting is allowed by permit only—if at all. Good management should, however, bring sage grouse numbers back to past levels and sportsmen will again have opportunity to pursue this unique game bird. Although sage grouse have contributed only 1 to 5% of the total upland harvest, they provide a unique type of diversity for Oregon Hunters.

TURKEY

The day I was waiting for had finally arrived and I was excited. I had been pestering Oregon Department of Fish and Wildlife's Steve Denny for several months to take me along on an early morning turkey count and he finally agreed. I was particularly excited because Steve is not only the district wildlife biologist for the Roseburg area and the foremost authority on Oregon turkeys, but he is also a superb turkey hunter in his own right. Prior to this field trip, I had never hunted or even see a wild turkey.

Daylight found us driving down an old logging road somewhere near the community of Tiller. Steve stopped the pickup on a pull-off that was surrounded by a dense forest of madrona, oak, and second-growth Douglas fir. "We planted some birds near here several years ago and they've really taken off. Hunters did very well here last season," Steve said. He pulled out an assortment of diaphragm turkey calls and selected his favorite. He then stepped out of the rig and gave a series of chuck,

A group of transplanted Rio Grande turkeys in Douglas County.(Photo courtesy Oregon Department of Fish and Wildlife)

chuck, chucks that he said was supposed to sound like a hen and would hopefully attract a love-sick gobbler. He called several times and then signaled me to step close and listen. I could hear the faint call of a lone gobbler. It took Steve a half hour of periodic calling but the big gobbler finally appeared with the rest of his flock on the edge of an opening about 75 yards away.

What a sight! There was the old tom, a dozen hens and a couple of "jakes" or young toms. We watched in silence as the flock moved along making strange noises and feeding contentedly. Every time Steve would call the old boy would stretch out his neck and give a shrill gobble. Finally the big fella spread his tail, fluffed up all his body feathers and began to strut in front of his favorite lady.

We moved on and Steve called in another flock before the morning ended. I was definitely impressed with Steve's knowledge as a biologist and hunter. Now I really wanted to bag a turkey.

My chance came about a month later as the turkey season opened on April 18. Steve had told me about a large flock of turkeys near Elkton and I was near the area early Saturday morning. I passed a farmhouse and continued until I came to the location Steve had described. Soon as I stepped out of my pickup I found tell-tale droppings and some fresh tracks in the soft mud. The birds were near and the hunt began.

I rubbed mud all over my face, grabbed my 20 gauge Model 12 Winchester and set up next to a tree several hundred yards away from the road. I called every 10 minutes for nearly an hour with no answer. I was just about to try one last time when a movement caught my eye. Closer inspection revealed it was a turkey cautiously approaching my stand and I froze. He was now only 50 yards away and I could plainly see it was a big tom—his bluish red head and four inch beard left no doubt.

He approached to about 30 yards and disappeared behind a log. I raised my shotgun, planning to put a 1 1/8 ounce charge of No. 6's in his neck and head area, when he next appeared from behind the log. With gun raised and safety off, a horrible thought occurred — was I on BLM land or on private property? That farmhouse wasn't too far away. Doubt filled my head and I lowered the gun. The thought of an irate landowner pressing trespass charges stopped me cold.

The big tom seemed to sense my doubt and exposed his entire body at less than 20 yards. I stood up and he was gone in a flash.

Totally frustrated, I made my way back to the pickup and reluctantly opened the ownership map like I should have done before the hunt. Just as I feared, I was hunting on BLM land and the bird was perfectly legal. So ended my first hunt and I didn't call in another bird the rest of the season.

A year has passed and strangely enough I don't feel badly about passing up that trophy bird. There will be other hunts and a good hunter will never pull the trigger if he has doubts.

HISTORY

The wild turkey is unique to North America. There is only one native species. However, six subspecies are recognized and four are common to the Unites States: Florida turkey, found only in Florida, Eastern turkey, of eastern and southern coastal woods, Rio Grande turkey, of southern Texas, and Merriam's turkey, found in the mountains of the southwestern United States.

With early settlement of the East Coast followed by progressive movement west, turkey numbers began to dwindle by the turn of the century. Heavy hunting and habitat loss caused the elimination of turkey in 19 of the 39 states which formerly boasted turkey populations.

The last several decades have seen a real comeback of the wild turkey throughout the nation. Restoration efforts have been successful through much of the turkey's native range. Wild turkeys have also been introduced outside their native ranges and all the states except Alaska now manage wild turkey populations.

Private individuals released turkeys in Oregon as early as 1899, none of which were successful. The Oregon Game Commission raised and released about 1,500 birds between 1926 and 1933 but the program was discontinued due to poor results. Game farm birds, which were

Retired Oregon Department of Fish and Wildlife biologist Bob Mace with a large tom taken in Oregon. (Photo courtesy Oregon Department of Fish and Wildlife)

predominantly Merriam's and the Eastern varieties, tended to become domesticated. The modern era of Oregon turkey management began in 1961. Fifty-eight Merriam's turkeys were released in three sites in eastern Oregon with good results. Rio Grande turkeys were released in 1975 in southwestern Oregon near Medford and are now thriving. From 1975 through 1987, over 600 Oregon Rio Grande turkeys were trapped and transplanted in 27 locations throughout eastern and western Oregon.

Limited hunting began in the spring of 1966 and has continued in April or May since. Hunting opportunities have expanded as populations have grown. In 1987 the entire state was opened to turkey hunting. Hunters are now required to apply as a controlled hunt application, but all who apply before the Feb. 15 deadline receive a tag. Turkey season currently begins in mid-April, continues for about three weeks, and the limit is one gobbler.

WHERE TO HUNT

According to Ken Durbin, Oregon Department of Fish and Wildlife's staff gamebird biologist, 1987 was Oregon's best season ever with 5,000 hunters taking 425 gobblers and having an overall success rate of 9%.

In 1987, turkeys were taken in eight different counties from all parts of the state. However, four counties accounted for the majority of total hunting pressure and birds killed.

Central Oregon's Wasco County had the heaviest hunting pressure and a fair success rate. Douglas County in southwestern Oregon had the second highest hunter numbers and also a high success rate. Both Jackson and Klamath Counties in the Medford and Klamath Falls area of southern Oregon had little hunting pressure but success rates were good.

The wild turkey is an extremely adaptable gamebird and does well in a variety of habitat types. Habitat in parts of Oregon where turkeys have been most successful is characterized by a mixture of oak, pine and other conifers, with a variety of sub-habitats including open meadows, wet areas and dense pole stands for nesting.

HOW TO HUNT

Turkey hunting is not as easy as it appears to be or as hard as some of the experts make it sound. Like other types of hunting, success depends on a variety of factors including area, weather and hunter perseverance. Learn as much as possible about turkey hunting — before you go — from books, tapes and personal interviews. Base your hunting selection on good research and preseason scouting. Don't hesitate to call your local Fish and Wildlife biologist and sport shop dealers for best hunting areas.

Learn to use a turkey call prior to the season opener. Talk to experts, read books and listen to tapes. A variety of calls are available but learn to master one and stick with it. Learn the basic hen call and stay with it until you develop confidence.

Wear as much camouflage clothing as necessary and break up your outline in a bush or against a tree when calling and waiting for a tom to come in. Always be alert and ready. They can appear at any time even if no response has been heard.

Rifles are not legal for turkey hunting in Oregon and a 20 gauge or larger shotgun must be used. Best turkey medicine is a 12 gauge loaded with No. 4,5, or 6 shot. Wait until the tom is within 30 yards and hopefully closer, then aim for the head and neck area.

They are definitely a thrill to hunt. Like one veteran turkey hunter once told me, "Once you call a big 20 pound gobbler, you're hooked on turkey hunting. You might even give up on big game hunting after that."

Thanks to Oregon Department of Fish and Wildlife's perseverance and never-quit attitude, turkey hunting in Oregon is here to stay.

BAND-TAIL PIGEON

Every year pigeon season would arrive Sept. 1 and I'd grab my 410 single shot and head for Sons of Norway Park along with the rest of my friends. This was the only pigeon flyway around and wasn't too far for m to ride my bike. It was located along the Necanicum River betwee

The author and father with limits of band-tailed pigeons shot at the Nehalem fly-away on the northern Oregon coast.

S.G. Johnson and Tom Savage with band-tails shot on the lower Umpqua River near Reedsport. Pigeons like the brackish water found in coastal estuaries.

Seaside and Gearhart and the birds came each day to drink the brackish water along the bay.

Around 50 to 100 birds would weave their way among the pine and spruce trees between 8 and 11 each morning. The problem was the hunters often nearly outnumbered the birds and competition was fierce. I soon learned that one 410 among many 12 gauges was a losing proposition. I found an old snag away from the rest that was good for at least one bird a day. Just as their feet would touch the branch and while their wings were still outstretched, I'd pull the trigger and down they would tumble. To me this was real sport.

One year my father asked my brother, Stan, and I to go with him and try to find the Nehalem flyway, about 20 miles to the south of Seaside. Westley Batterson, a biologist for the old Game Commission and Oregon's foremost authority on the band-tailed pigeon, had told my Dad that more birds were counted at Nehalem than any place in Oregon. He had banded hundreds of birds at Nehalem trying to learn more about their age structure and migration patterns.

We arrived early but had to walk a cow trail for a quarter mile until we reached Nehalem Bay. What a beautiful setting! A large stand of spruce and pine trees came right to the high tide mark. The bay was deep blue with flocks of widgeon and pintail bobbing here and there. In the distance were the sun-lit sand dunes of the Nehalem spit which was lined with rows of drift wood. We noticed a few driftwood blinds and plucked pigeon feathers were here and there. This was the spot and there were only a few other hunters.

We spread out along the bay front just as the first flock of a dozen birds arrived. A stiff breeze was blowing so they came in from the bay low and fast. I now had a 20 gauge double and Stan and dad each shot 12 gauge full choked pumps. I selected the lead bird, took a three foot lead, and sent an ounce of 6's skyward. A puff of feathers and down he tumbled. Stan and dad also connected. In a couple of hours, we all had our eight bird limits and a tradition was started. I've hunted dozens of small flyways all along the Oregon Coast, but Nehalem has always been my favorite.

The band-tail in Oregon is primarily a bird of the Coast Range although it is also seen in the Cascades and occasionally in eastern Oregon. They like both oaks and conifers and rugged country with steep slopes and canyons. They are a migratory bird and they arrive from the South in May and stay to feed and rear their young through the summer and into October, when they again move south.

There are relatively few Oregon sportsmen who pursue these half pound game birds. Only 10,000 to 15,000 hunters take anywhere from 50,000 to 120,000 band-tails annually. The usual bag limit of eight has been reduced and the seasons shortened in recent years in an effort to increase band-tail populations. The results look encouraging. It would be a shame to see these wonderful game birds go the route of the passenger pigeon.

WHERE TO HUNT

Band-tail harvest is spread fairly even along the entire coast as well as the lower Columbia region. Band-tail have a unique physiological requirement that necessitates visits to mineral springs or coastal estuaries to obtain calcium from brackish water during that period when they are producing "pigeon milk" to feed their young. This is where most pigeons are shot in Oregon and where most of my hunting has occurred. There are numerous esturine flyways along the entire coast line. Stop at any sport shop in any coastal town and they will tell you where the local flyways are. The scenic setting of these isolated shooting areas is usually worth the hike to reach them. Most are situated along a coastal river or tidal bay where spruce trees and driftwood meet. I've hunted the entire coast of Oregon and some of my favorite pigeon flyways are as follows: Nehalem Bay, Tillamook Bay near Bay City, Tahkenitch Lake outlet near Florence, Umpqua Bay near Gardiner, and Sixes River near Port Orford. Dozens more exist and with a little effort you can find them.

Band-tails feed on Cascara or Chitum berries and a hunter can do quite well if he can locate a mountain pass where birds are going to or returning from these feeding areas. Some hunters simply drive around looking for feeding pigeons or birds sitting gracefully atop bent over hemlock trees.

Wherever you choose to hunt pigeons in Oregon, it is important to know that shooting is best in the morning between 8:00 and 11:00 a.m. A hunter can occasionally find mountain passes and feeding areas where evening shooting is excellent but they are hard to come by. A low-hanging fog that is common along the Oregon coast and will often prevent band-tails from arriving early in the morning at many fly-ways. Be patient and wait for the fog to lift. Birds will arrive as late as two in the afternoon when the fog finally begins to lift.

Early September is best hunting and band-tails like sunny weather. They fly very little in the heavy rain. Persistent rain for a week or so will move most birds south to California, seeking warmer temperatures.

Very little has been written about band-tail hunting so I will briefly discuss guns and hunting ethics. Pigeons are a tough bird and require a dense pattern with fairly large shot. A 12 gauge in full or modified choke or a 20 gauge in full choke is good band-tail medicine. Never use shot smaller than 7 1/2's and 6's or even 5's are a good idea. Smaller shot will only wound or cripple these birds.

Pigeons are often difficult to find once you knock one down because of the thick coastal brush. When a bird is downed, extreme care must be taken to mark it well. Many hunters say it is unethical to hunt pigeons without a good dog because losses are so high without one. Unless you hunt open terrain with little cover, a dog is a necessity. Band-tails provide such a wonderful sporting experience that it is a shame to waste even one.

SEASON

Pigeon season traditionally opens Sept. 1 and continues the entire month. Pre-season counts have been low in recent years and on more than one occasion, the season length has been cut in half, beginning Sept. 15 and ending Sept. 30.

JACKSNIPE

It was one of those days that all duck hunters have dreams about, actually more like nightmares. My long-time friend and hunting partner, Jon Weber and I, had planned this duck hunt for several weeks. We arrived at the south jetty near Astoria at least an hour before sunrise and had to pack three dozen decoys and drag a small skiff a quarter mile up and down over rolling sand dunes. Our decoys were set and hopes were high until the rising sun revealed a bluebird sky and no wind.

Jon broke the silence after an hour or so. "Did you bring any 7 1/2's with you?"

"Yeh, I brought a box just in case we got into some teal," I replied.

"There should be some jacksnipe out here. Let's give that a try," he

Eric Johnson with jacksnipe near Gardiner on the central Oregon coast. His snipe gun is a model 12 Winchester in modified choke.

Jacksnipe prefer moist grasslands and scattered clumps of cover. They often hold tight for the gun and a double, bored modified and improved cylinder is about right.

said. That sounded great to me so we pulled the decoys and went after snipe. Several days of rain had moistened the sand and left pockets of water here and there. That brings worms near the surface where snipe probe for them with their three inch bills.

We worked our way through the dunes about 50 yards apart, hunting each isolated marsh area. It seemed like every little depression that held any moisture had snipe. Sometimes a single, but more often a small flock would jump, all sounding off with a warning of "screech-screech-screech" as they zig-zagged skyward. I kept missing while Jon would hit every other bird or so. Soon he yelled, "Shoot quick before they start that damned zig-zagging." I followed his advice and finally dropped three birds before my half box was gone. We finished the hunt with eight birds between us — half a limit, but both agreed that jacksnipe had turned a near disaster into a pleasant hunting experience.

The jacksnipe or Wilson's snipe is considered by many hunters, including me, to be Oregon's most challenging game bird. Although they are similar in appearance to their eastern cousin, the woodcock, the smaller jacksnipe provides a unique hunting experience.

Wilson's snipe are widely distributed in Oregon. Because they prefer wet meadows, marshes and bogs, two-thirds of Oregon's annual average harvest, about 16,000 birds, are taken in western Oregon.

Relatively few sportsmen go hunting strictly for jacksnipe. Most snipe are taken incidentally by duck hunters as they walk to or from their duck blinds or while they are jump-shooting around drainage ditches. As a kid growing up around the Seaside-Astoria area, my first few snipe were taken in conjunction with duck hunting. I quickly learned that No. 4 shot in a heavy duck load made frequent kills just about impossible.

I now go hunting specifically for jacksnipe and enjoy every minute of the hunt. These dove-sized birds will test even the best of wing shots. When flushed, snipe fly low and erratically. Their zig-zag flight pattern makes even straight-away shots quite difficult. For a real challenge, try pass shooting at these quarter-pounders as they fly overhead.

The perfect quail gun is the perfect snipe gun. Use small shot like 7 1/2, 8, or 9's in a small gauge shotgun. A modified choke is fine. However, improved cylinder is often times even better. My favorite snipe gun is a 20 gauge, double-bored, improved cylinder and modified.

WHERE TO GO

Snipe are found throughout Oregon but western Oregon, especially the moist coastal areas, are where snipe hunting is best. Look for shallow standing water in fields or marshes where some hiding cover is available. Find a large field with one or two inches of water and clumps of green wiregrass and you'll likely find jacksnipe. If you don't find any birds, don't give up. Snipe are migratory by nature and are here one week and gone the next.

Tillamook County in northwestern Oregon probably has Oregon's finest jacksnipe habitat. The dairy industry provides an abundance of pastured fields and heavy winter rains yield plenty of standing water. The tidal marshs around Tillamook Bay are also excellent snipe country.

Southwestern Oregon also has fine snipe hunting. The Umpqua, Coos, and Coquille valleys are great prospects and consistent snipe producers. Fern Ridge Reservoir, close to Eugene, is a first-rate choice for jacksnipe. Some of the largest concentrations of snipe I have ever hunted have been around the perimeter of Fern Ridge Reservoir. I was within rifle shot of Oregon's second largest city and, on more than one occasion, the only hunter after snipe!

Wherever you choose to hunt jacksnipe in Oregon, be ready for a real test of your wing shooting ability. Take a box of shells, and come home with the usual limit of eight birds, and consider yourself a very good shot. Competition for these "western woodcocks" is practically nonexistent and they are fine table fare as well. What more could a hunter ask for?

HUNTING SEASON

Jacksnipe are a migratory bird and maximum season lengths are man-dated by the federal government. Season lengths and opening dates generally coincide with duck season, which normally starts in mid-October.

The author's mother, Margaret, with a dove shot near a wheatfield a short distance from Madras in central Oregon. She shoots a 20 gauge Winchester model 12 with a modified choke—the ideal dove gun.

MOURNING DOVE

The memory of my most recent dove hunt still remains clear in detail, as though it happened only yesterday. A friend and I were hunting the wheat fields near Maupin, Oregon, that traditionally yields large number of doves. We had both taken our places, I by a juniper snag and my partner near a telephone line on the perimeter of the field. Frozen ground was all around us as we waited for sunrise and wondered if this early frost might push the birds south as it often does.

With the first warming rays of sunshine came the first flock of 30 or 40 doves. Although doves fly at only moderate speeds, they appear much faster as they twist and dive through the air. They streaked along the power line and my partner got a clean double. The flock flared and came my way. They spotted my dove decoy and came right in to the juniper. I felt quite lucky to drop one bird as they darted in with wings whirling.

Shooting slowed down about 10:00 a.m. and we moved out to jump-shoot spooky birds as they fed in the wheat stubble. Rising doves make tough shots. Some of our birds were taken at 55 to 65 paces. They are fragile birds and a single body hit will bring them down. We finished up our 10 bird limit that evening as they came to water near a small irrigation pond. It was a wonderful hunt but me and my 20 gauge shotgun were both tired — I had shot over two boxes of shells to get my limit.

There are 15,000 to 20,000 Oregon hunters who hunt these "grey streaks" each season and they harvest from 150,000 to 210,000 birds annually. No matter where you hunt doves in Oregon, success or failure depends on the weather conditions. An early cold snap or rain storms will drive birds south to California and fast. If the weather cooperates, good shooting can be had until mid-September or later.

WHERE TO HUNT

Doves in Oregon are found in the Willamette Valley and east of the Cascades. Mourning doves on the Oregon Coast are extremely rare indeed. In 20 years I've only seen one dove near the ocean.

The food of doves is almost entirely weed seeds and waste grain, particularly wheat. The entire Willamette Valley has excellent dove hunting. However, southwestern Oregon, especially the Medford area, has the best dove shooting in the state according to Rick Werner, district wildlife biologist for the Medford area. The wheat fields of northcentral Oregon, near Redmond, Prineville, and Maupin are great dove areas if the weather cooperates.

Mourning doves usually feed from daybreak until around noon and field hunting is best at that time. Doves are dependent on water and drink at least once a day. Find the only pond near some grain fields, set a decoy or two in a tree or on a fence, and get ready for good shooting.

Doves are a hard bird to hit but the 4 to 6 ounce birds come down easily when you do connect. Small shot is the rule for dove hunting — 7 1/2 or 8's are good choices. A full choke is best for jump-shooting birds from grain fields or pass shooting as they come in. An improved cylinder or modified choke is best if you are hunting under decoys or waiting by a pond for shots will be close in both cases.

SEASONS

The season usually opens Sept. 1 and continues the entire month. The bag limit is normally 10 doves per day.

Chapter 10

WATERFOWL

We were snow goose hunting at Summer Lake in southcentral Oregon and everything seemed perfect. I had called Oregon Department of Fish and Wildlife's area manager, Bill Smith, to find out the daily bird-per-hunter average. It was good, over two geese per gun. The first major freeze-up, which drives snow geese south, had not occurred yet and well over 100,000 birds were on the lake. We were even lucky enough to get reservations at the only motel in town.

The mile-long walk out to the end of the "Bull Dike" and layers of down did little to warm us up. That cold November wind knifed into every little crack in our clothing and numbed our noses and cheeks. The persistent icy wind kept tears flowing from my eyes. We huddled against the dike and waited for sunrise.

The sun finally crested the eastern shore and geese began to stir. The noise level from thousands of nervous snow geese was overwhelming. "This is great," dad said. "This strong wind will force the birds to fly low and we'll get some good shooting. Go set those sacks out quick." I wandered about 100 yards in back of the dike and set out three dozen white paper sacks, a cheap but effective decoy for snows. Then the waiting game began.

Most birds were flying too high for us even though we were both using Winchester Model 12's with 1 1/2 ounce loads of No. 2's. Once in a while we would hear a tremendous roar from down below and a goose would fall as if struck by lightning from what looked to be 100 yards up. It had to be a 10 gauge magnum.

We had not waited more than a half hour when we noticed a flock circle our "decoys", set their wings, and start to drop down. Snow geese are five pound birds with extremely large wing spans. They appear much

Oregon's waterfowl hunting is terribly underrated. Next to California, Oregon has some of the finest duck and goose hunting to be found in the western United States.

closer than they are and holding fire was a very tough assignment. Finally dad gave the signal and we both jumped up, guns blazing. We dropped four geese and by 11 a.m. had our five bird limits. The memories from that particular experience have taken me back for several return hunts and each time I've not been disappointed.

Whether you are decoying mallards on Tillamook Bay, jump-shooting woodducks in the Willamette Valley, or pass-shooting snow geese at Summer Lake, you will search long and hard to find better duck and goose shooting than is available in Oregon.

I have hunted waterfowl all over the western United States including the great Copper River Delta in Alaska. It is my firm conviction that Oregon has some of the best duck and goose hunting to be found west of the Mississippi. Oregon is, however, definitely second best compared to California in terms of birds harvested. "Most of Oregon, with the exception of the Columbia Basin and the Willamette Valley, is a transition area that waterfowl use for a migration route on their way south," states the Oregon Department Fish and Wildlife's district wildlife biologist in Roseburg, Steve Denney. "That is why Oregon hasn't got the reputation of California." That, however, does not mean Oregon is inferior in terms of good quality waterfowl hunting. Oregon has a greater variety of habitat types and it doesn't have the hunter density of California.

Waterfowl hunting is a very popular sport in the Beaver State. Each year 50,000 to 65,000 hunters harvest from 500,000 to 1,000,000 ducks and up to 90,000 geese.

More than this large annual harvest, the thing that makes Oregon such a great place for waterfowl hunting is the tremendous variety of habitat available for ducks and geese throughout the state. From the brackish tidewaters of the balmy coastal area, to the high desert grain fields of northeastern Oregon or the flooded farm fields of Malheur Lake, Oregon has all the necessary requirements for great waterfowl hunting.

WHERE TO HUNT

Oregon's **coastal bays** or estuaries are a well kept waterfowling secret. These unique water bodies, where fresh and salt water meet, are a tremendous source of nutrients that attract tens of thousands of waterfowl each year. Lots of ducks and relatively few geese is the general rule on the Oregon Coast. Black Brant, a marine goose, are found in many of the estuaries, but numbers are low and hunting opportunities quite limited. Duck hunters will, however, find excellent shooting along the Oregon coast, especially from Coos Bay north to the Columbia River. Access to hunt the numerous bays and tide-flats is seldom a problem as they are all in public ownership.

Some mention should be made regarding food preference and diet of coastal ducks inhabiting esturine environments. Many hunters complain that coastal ducks are not fit to eat — even mallards and pintail. It is true that coastal ducks consume a higher percent of animal matter than do grain-fed inland birds. According to Jay Long, retired wildlife instructor at Oregon State University, this does change the flavor of the flesh slightly, giving it a strong taste. I personally cannot tell the difference between a grain-fed mallard and a coastal bird if both are soaked overnight in salt water.

Coos Bay, the Coquille Valley, Umpqua Bay and the Siuslaw Estuary are excellent duck hunting destinations. There always seems to be good numbers of local mallards, teal and widgeon early in the season. However, shooting is best in December and January when northern birds are forced south. The Willamette Valley will usually have one good cold spell each year that lasts a week or two. Most water bodies freeze up and those birds head for the coast looking for open water. This is when coastal duck hunting is at its best. Ducks seem unwary and eager to decoy.

The cold weather also brings bluebill down from the north. The lower Umpqua River and Siltcoos Lake, just north of Reedsport, has the finest late winter bluebill shooting found anywhere in Oregon. It is not uncommon to view rafts of bluebill numbering 5,000 to 10,000 according to Pete Perrin, Oregon Department of Fish and Wildlife biologist in Coos Bay. The best hunting method is to set up with 100 or more decoys. Jump-shooting from a camouflaged sneak boat can also be very successful. December is the best month and a strong west wind combined with an outgoing tide is the perfect situation. Bluebill usually concentrate on the Umpqua River 5 to 10 miles east of Reedsport. Put your boat in a quarter-mile upstream and silently drift into the center of a flock. When the time is right and you do decide to raise up, don't be surprised if you are surrounded by 1,000 or more bluebill. Believe me, for the next three or four minutes, the action is nonstop!

Yaquina Bay at Newport and Siletz Bay near Lincoln City offers fair to good duck shooting depending on weather conditions up north and in the Willamette Valley. The only drawback for hunting these two estuaries is that hunting pressure can become heavy at times.

If I were asked to choose my favorite place to duck hunt, it would be Tillamook Bay. The reason I am so fond of this estuary is because it is a very large bay that attracts great numbers of ducks and hunting pressure is quite low. According to retired Oregon Game Commission wildlife biologist Wesley Batterson, widgeon, teal, and bufflehead are the most common birds on the bay. Mallards do not use this estuary in great numbers. The best areas to hunt over decoys are in the marshy tide-flats of the upper bay. The Trask, Wilson, and Tillamook Rivers enter the bay there and this fresh water habitat creates excellent duck shooting. Sneak along the bay during high tide during a harsh winter storm and you will find the best jump-shooting available. Several public boat ramps are available at various locations around the bay.

Oregon's coastal estuaries provide superb duck shooting, especially late in the season. My son, Eric, with a couple of bluebill shot on the Umpqua Bay. The Umpqua River and Siltcoos Lake have the best bluebill shooting in the state.

Oregon Department of Fish and Wildlife biologist, Craig Ely, with a couple of snow geese shot near Summer Lake. Summer Lake has the best snow goose shooting in the state as well as excellent duck hunting. (Credit Craig Ely)

Nehalem Bay, about 20 miles north of Tillamook, also offers excellent duck hunting with only limited hunter numbers. This bay is probably the most picturesque estuary on the Oregon Coast and I personally have never been skunked while hunting there. Best shooting occurs up-bay opposite the little community of Wheeler. Access is no problem as there are several fine boat ramps around the bay.

The **lower Columbia River** from Astoria to Portland has historically yielded more ducks and geese than anywhere in Oregon. I grew up duck hunting the islands along the Columbia River around Astoria, Knappa, and Swenson. Mallards, pintail and a few geese are the rule in that area. This is waterfowling in the traditional sense. As you explore the islands, channels and sloughs, you'll find quality old duck shacks and elegant duck blinds. The area just looks great for duck and goose hunting and it really is! There are several good boat ramps around the area, but the John Day River ramp about five miles east of Astoria along Highway 30 is right in the middle of great hunting.

The Sauvie Island Wildlife Area is an intensively utilized public recreation area only 10 miles from Portland and managed by the Oregon Department of Fish and Wildlife. It is 12,000 acres in size and managed almost exclusively for waterfowl. About 10,000 hunters harvest approximately 20,000 ducks and 1,000 or so geese each year in the shadow of Oregon's largest city. This is truly a tribute to progressive scientific wildlife management.

Much of the Columbia River to the east of Portland is a wildlife refuge and hunting is not allowed. It is a remarkable sight to view thousands of ducks and geese resting peacefully along the mighty Columbia's diverse shoreline. These geese make daily flights inland to feed in the vast expanses of wheatland. Excellent pass shooting can be had on the high bluffs from Hood River east to The Dalles, Biggs Junction, and Rufus.

Umatilla and Cold Springs National Wildlife Refuges near Hermiston, can have excellent waterfowl shooting. Hunting is best later in the season when northern birds arrive. According to Dave Sill with the U.S. Fish and Wildlife Service in Portland, Umatilla Refuge has a large number of developed blinds available by drawing. Hunting is best when the wind really howls. Goose hunting can be superb at McKay National Wildlife Refuge, which surrounds McCay Reservoir near Pendleton. The best shoot I've ever experienced on large Canadian honkers occurred on a stormy day near the south end of McKay Reservoir. Strong winds forced the birds to fly 30 to 40 yards high and we had our limits in no time shooting magnum 5's.

Open water can be a scarce commodity on the **east side** in the late season. **Creeks and rivers** are the last to freeze and jump-shooting is often very productive. There are literally hundreds of streams for the hunter to choose from. However, several are worth special note. An Oregon Department of Fish and Wildlife biologist from Baker, Vic Coggins, once suggested I try chukar hunting along the rimrocks of the Burnt and Powder Rivers. We did great on chukar but also shot limits of grain-fed mallards along both rivers. To the south, the Malheur River is always a good bet when the ice begins to form and the snow starts to fly. Much of the land along these creeks and rivers is in private ownership, so be sure to acquire the necessary permission.

Southern Oregon offers some of the best waterfowling to be found in the state. Summer Lake is best known for snow geese but the duck shooting can be great and fair numbers of Canada geese use the lake. Malheur Lake is best known for its excellent duck hunting but also has fine shooting for Canadian honkers. The Klamath Falls area near the California border offers the best Canada Goose hunting in the state — hands down.

The **Willamette Valley**, from Portland south to Cottage Grove, is the most populated section of the state. Despite heavy human numbers, duck and goose hunting can be very good. There are hundreds of creeks, ponds, swamps, lakes and reservoirs throughout the valley that attract northern mallards, pintail, teal, and are home to a resident population of Dushey Canada geese.

The Willamette River basically begins south of Eugene and meanders the entire length of the Willamette Valley to join the Columbia River at Portland. This may be the most underrated water body in the state in terms of duck numbers and hunting opportunity. I personally have made several duck hunts from a drifting canoe with excellent results. Most birds were jumped as I silently drifted down river; however, a good decoy set in the adjacent side channels can be deadly. I was always impressed by the fact that few if any other hunters were encountered during these hunts. Think of it, 130 miles of great duck hunting opportunity with hardly any hunting pressure.

Fern Ridge Wildlife area, near Eugene, is fast becoming one of the most popular waterfowl areas in the Willamette Valley. It is 5,010 acres in size with 15 developed blinds. Most hunting is by permit entry.

DUCKS UNLIMITED

No discussion of waterfowl hunting in Oregon would be complete without mention of the great waterfowl conservation group, Ducks Unlimited. They began in 1937 and have since raised over $337 million and completed 2,900 wetland projects throughout the United State and Canada designed to improve or rehabilitate waterfowl wetland habitat.

Ducks Unlimited is represented by 60 chapters in Oregon. They recently spent over $45,000 alone to rebuild nesting islands at Summer Lake that were lost in the 1964 flood. At this writing, Ducks Unlimited is working on a plan to improve waterfowl habitat at Dean's Creek Elk Viewing Area near Reedsport and add nesting islands at the Fern Ridge Wildlife

Area near Eugene. According to Mike Duval, south coast area chairman for Ducks Unlimited, a total of $30,000 has been raised and donated for these two projects. Ducks Unlimited represents a bright light in the future of ducks and geese in the state of Oregon.

Jackrabbit hunting is great exercise and the hunter can burn plenty of powder. Beginners can use shotguns; however, more experienced hunters prefer a semi-automatic 22 like this Browning.

Chapter 11

VARMINTS

The letter I was waiting for had finally arrived and I was more than anxious to open it. Two weeks earlier, a friend and I were driving along a graveled country road within rifle-shot of Redmond, Oregon, when we spotted a rather large, brown animal scramble across a lush green alfalfa field and disappear into a rock pile. We stopped the rig and within seconds two sets of binoculars were trained on the neatly stacked pile of volcanic rock.

"What do ya suppose it was, a badger?" asked Larry.

"Either that or a marmot," I replied. "I've heard this is a good area for rockchucks." In a couple of minutes the mystery was solved as a pot-bellied groundhog crawled out to sun himself on a flat rock. Upon closer inspection, several other half-hidden figures could be seen and all were enjoying one of central Oregon's first warm spring days.

We were anxious to try for permission to hunt and soon were knocking on the front door of a ranch house whose best days were 20 years in the past. There was no answer and, not wanting to wind up in the local jail on trespass charges, we both decided to write a letter asking permission to hunt the group of marmots we had just spotted.

Quite frankly, I was surprised the rancher had taken time to reply to my letter of inquiry and even more surprised at his answer. It was short in length and to the point. "You boys are welcome to hunt my land, and we've got lots of chucks. Don't forget your fish poles cause I've got several ponds full of bass and catfish."

The next weekend found Larry and I back at the Redmond ranch and ready for our first ever rockchuck hunt. I couldn't understand why the rancher was so happy to have us hunt the marmots until he explained that one 10 pound chuck will eat 500 pounds of prime alfalfa during the course of a season. Raising beef, not rockchucks, was his business!

As we moved out across the fields of ankle-high grass, I could quickly see that more than just a few marmots had set up residence. Each rock pile, created from earlier land clearing, was literally alive with those yellow-bellied rodents. We stationed ourselves about 200 yards from the first rock pile and flipped a coin for the first shot.

Luck of the flip was mine and my chosen target was a great yellow chuck whose size and weight were comparable to that of a young cocker spaniel. These chucks obviously had not been hunted much but this big fellow got wind of the danger and dove for cover. Within a few minutes he exposed himself again. Now only his head and neck offered a shot. My 222 Remington barked and the 50 grain handload found its mark.

Next was Larry's turn and his 22-250 proved to be deadly accurate. Lightning seemed to strike each marmot as he squeezed off four hits in a row. We continued to work that cluster of rocks until no more targets remained.

We wandered from one rock pile to another until we burned up 40 rounds apiece. With no more ammo, we reluctantly headed back for the rig a mile or so away. We sent about 50 rockchucks to those big alfalfa fields in the sky that day and have since returned to hunt that central Oregon ranch many times.

I have been a hunter since childhood. I can remember wearing out three BB guns before receiving my first .22 at age eight. As a teenager, I remember how depressed I would get when duck season ended as that signaled the end of hunting season. I soon learned to drive a car and that was when I began to realize that hunting season didn't have to end with the coming of the new year. I began to understand that Oregon's diverse climate and topography offered a variety of small-game, off-season hunting opportunities. From tiny pine squirrels to deer-killing coyotes, I've hunted most of the small game that inhabit Oregon.

ROCKCHUCKS

Western marmots, also known as rockchucks or whistlers, are found only east of the Cascades. Marmots are most numerous in the northeast corner of the state, especially near La Grande and Baker. The Bend-Redmond area of central Oregon also has fairly high marmot densities and is where most of my hunting experience have taken place. Isolated pockets of rockchucks are spread all over eastern Oregon; however, huntable numbers can be hard to find.

Locating an area that has plenty of marmots to shoot and gaining legal hunting access are the most difficult aspects of rockchuck hunting. Stop and chat with sport shops or, easier yet, phone them up and inquire as to where the best chuck areas are located. Most dealers are very cooperative and oftentimes they will give you names of ranchers who might allow

Rock piles, in and around green fields, are where you will find marmots throughout central Oregon. The Three Sisters Mountains provide a scenic backdrop.

hunting. Marmots come out of hibernation in April and May depending on weather conditions. They need plenty of grass or alfalfa to forage on and adequate cover such as rock formations or fencerows to escape from predators and hide from man. Unfortunately, most of the prime marmot hunting is associated with cattle ranches. Talking a rancher into allowing shooting near his prize cattle is indeed a delicate situation with results not always what you'd like. I once approached a tough-looking rancher and asked, "Do you mind if I ask permission to hunt rockchucks on your land?"

"No, I don't mind if you ask," was his reply.

There was a confused moment of silence and I asked, "Well, can I have permission?"

A simple "No, you can't," was his reply. Then he politely smiled and went back to his work.

First impressions are important in the permission game and the approach you use can gain you hours of mind-relaxing pleasure or send you down the road frustrated and wishing you had said the right thing. When you approach a landowner, be polite and courteous. Never go to the door with a beer in one hand and a rifle in the other. Show the fellow that you are a conscientious hunter who will never shoot near his stock, break down fences or leave gates open. Should you be lucky enough to gain access to a ranch with good hunting, a thank-you in the form of a cold six-

Rockchuck hunting requires a flat-shooting rifle and a steady hand. The author readies for a long shot near Redmond in central Oregon.

pack is a refreshing treat to a thirsty rancher. You might also consider sending a thank-you card upon returning from the hunt. Treat folks right and they will often reward you with future hunting privileges.

Rockchucks can be hunted with anything from a .22 pistol to a 375 H & H Magnum depending on how often the chucks have been shot at, the terrain you are hunting, and your specific hunting desires. More marmots have probably been killed by ranch hands or farm boys with open-sighted .22's than anything else. If I am working an area where the chucks have had little hunting pressure, I use my Winchester Model 52 Sporter and try only head shots with hi-speed hollow points. I use a 3 power scope and can make sure kills out to about 100 yards. I prefer to use a rimfire on chucks because the light report won't send them running to the next county like other hot-shot centerfires. I have often shot six or eight rockchucks from one vantage point only 50 yards from my target.

The .22 WMR is an excellent choice for the beginning chuck hunter or the sportsman who wants centerfire performance from a rimfire. A box of 50 is about three times the cost of a box of .22 rifle shells. However, you are rewarded with twice the muzzle energy and flatter trajectory. My scope-sighted Model 61 Winchester will kill chucks cleanly out to 150 yards.

If rock whistlers have been hunted hard, a .22 centerfire is the only way to go. The crack of a rifle or slam of a car door will send chucks scrambling for cover and a 200 yard shot is considered close under these conditions. Over the years, I've used three .22 center-fires for marmots: .22 Hornet, 222 Remington and the 22-250 Remington. The Hornet is good to 200 yards, the 222 a fine killer to 275 yards and dead chucks to 400 yards are possible with the 22-250. No matter which caliber you choose, I suggest using SX or super explosive bullets to reduce the odds of ricochet. Handloads must be kept under 3,500 FPS or the paper thin jackets will literally disintegrate in mid-air and never reach the intended target.

The rifle you choose for rockchuck hunting must be capable of fine accuracy. It should put five shots into an inch of 100 yards and hopefully less. Remember, an inch at 100 yards equates to three inches at 300 yards and could easily account for a clean miss on even the largest marmot.

Good optics are a must in varmint hunting — you can shoot only as good as you can see. A 6 power scope should be considered the minimum and my preference is a 8 power with a duplex reticle. Carry a light pair of compact binoculars — it is much easier to raise 6 ounce binoculars than a 10 pound rifle when scanning fields for several hours.

GREYDIGGERS

Greydiggers, also known as California or Columbian ground squirrels, are a grayish-brown, foot-long rodent that inhabit the entire state. However the highest densities are found west of the Cascades. They provide the only real form of varmint hunting that western Oregon residents can hunt from April, when they first come out of hibernation, to October when they again join the ranks of the winter-time sleepers. As a lad growing up on the Oregon Coast, greydiggers were the closest thing to East Coast woodchuck hunting I'd experience until I turned 16 and could drive to eastern Oregon. They provided endless hours of entertainment. I'm sure it made me a better shot and improved my overall hunting skills. The sure-kill-zone of an adult greydigger is 2 inches by 2 inches and quite a challenge to a youngster using an open-sighted .22 single-shot.

These "mini-woodchucks" are a burrowing animal that like to be near cover such as rocks, logs or stumps where they can run for safety and climb up high for a good look around. On the coast they are frequently found in association with logged-over units that were cut at least two years prior. They particularly like burned over logs and stumps. Greydiggers seem to prefer the openness and abundance of grass seeds and berries that logging produces. Diggers are seldom found in logging units with brush or trees higher than three or four feet. I have shot greydiggers in logged-over areas throughout the Coast Range from Astoria to Brookings and thoroughly enjoyed each experience.

The Willamette Valley has an abundance of these ground squirrels that cause farmers many problems. They invade grainfields, gardens, fruit and

Greydiggers or California ground squirrels provide plenty of spring and summer shooting action for west-side Oregonians. The author's kids, Eric and Kai, with greydiggers shot near Elkton in Douglas County.

nut orchards causing untold damage. Many a horse, sheep and cow has broke a leg in a hole dug by greydiggers.

Landowners will often give permission to hunt these pests if you ask and assure them you are a safe and conscientious hunter. I know a sheep rancher near Roseburg who has allowed me to thin down his greydigger population for the past eight years. The green pastures and rolling hills are dotted with oak groves and old stumps. This is perfect digger country and very scenic as it bounds the picturesque Umpqua River. Each spring before the grass gets too high, I take my rifle and spend many wonderful afternoons stalking greydiggers, popping primers, and relieving all stress and tension. If I shoot 10 or more it's been a good hunt and over the years I've probably taken over 500 from those fields. It's great entertainment and I've helped out the rancher.

Good calibers for greydiggers range from the .22 rimfire to your favorite deer rifle. Large-bore rifles are fine for the wide-open spaces. However, around populated areas it is better to stick with the .22 long rifle, the .22 magnum, and my overall favorite for greydiggers, the .22 Hornet. Which ever rifle you use, be sure it is accurate. They are a small target that often won't give you a second chance.

JACK RABBITS

Jack rabbits can be found in most lowland desert areas of central and eastern Oregon. Sagebrush and jack rabbits are practically inseparable, especially if alfalfa or hay fields are nearby. Rabbit populations are cyclic and fluxuate from year to year. I've hunted hot spots where rabbits were so plentiful that I couldn't load my rifle fast enough. I returned the next year, hiked all day, and never caught sight of a bounding bunny. Nature's method of population control makes long range rabbit hunting predictions nearly impossible. A tried and proven method for locating good rabbit hunting is to count the number of dead rabbits you encounter along the highways you drive. When you begin to find two to four "flat rabbits" per mile, chances are the hunting will be good. Jack rabbit hunting is pretty good when you get shots at a dozen rabbits every half hour or so.

A favorite and consistent spot for rabbit hunting is the Fort Rock — Christmas Valley area and local ranchers are happy to have you lower the number of rabbits feeding on their valuable crops of alfalfa. I have occasionally found pretty fair jack hunting around Bend and Redmond. However, as the people population swells, it becomes more difficult to gain the necessary hunting permission. I have had excellent rabbit hunting around Summer Lake and recently heard talk of good shooting near Boardman, north of Pendleton.

Like many first-time rabbit hunters, I began hunting these long-eared, desert speedsters with a shotgun. I used a 20 gauge with high-based No. 4 shot and had good results as long as I limited my shots to 40 yards or less. I soon discovered that gunning jacks with a scattergun offered little challenge and decided to try running bunnies with a .22 rifle. This proved to be real sport and is the method I still prefer today.

A .22 auto with opensights is the way to go for this business — a scope is too slow for running jacks. Any .22 autoloader will do but my idea of the perfect rabbit gun is the Browning automatic .22. This outfit rarely jams, weighs only 4 1/2 pounds, and has perfect balance. You can burn up 500 rounds of ammo on a good day and if you are lucky enough to knock off 10 bouncing rabbits, consider yourself a good shot.

Hunting jack rabbits with your favorite big game rifle can really sharpen your reflexes and shooting skills. The best shot I've ever seen on running deer is a friend who makes several trips a year to the Oregon deserts specifically to hunt running jacks with his scoped 30-06. I tried it once and that was enough. I enjoy a challenge but hits were just too few and far between to keep my interest up.

The ultimate challenge is hunting running jacks with a pistol. I recall asking a rancher near Bend for permission to try for rabbits on his land. He was happy to allow hunting and asked what weapons we were going to hunt with. Semi-automatic .22's was our answer. "Why don't you give em a chance? The only thing I hunt rabbits with is a .22 automatic pistol."

That was 20 years ago and we took his advice with a grain of salt. My wife and I ran into a lot of jacks near Reno, Nevada a couple of years ago and I decided to try my .22 Colt Woodsman. I shot 200 rounds and to my surprise, nailed five of those evasive desert hares. I definitely would not, however, recommend a pistol as a tool for rabbit population control.

Some skeptics might question the sanity of a person who would plan a vacation for and travel long distances just to hunt a rodent that most folks consider only coyote food. The excitement I feel as I wander over miles of sagebrush with a good rifle is truly exhilarating. I always feel my heart pace quicken as a big jack breaks from cover, running full tilt as he dodges in and out of the protective cover. My .22 spits lead and dust kicks up usually a foot or two behind the evasive target. After 10 or 15 miles and a half day of hunting, my lungs feel full of spicy desert air, my legs are weary, and I am thoroughly content. That's what I call therapeutic entertainment.

COTTONTAIL RABBITS

Isolated populations of cottontail are found here and there throughout Oregon. However, huntable numbers reside east of the Cascade Mountains. Look for these two pound, bouncing balls of fur in dry arid country with adequate amounts of cover. Jack rabbits rely on good eyesight and speed from their long legs to out-distance predators. Cottontail are also fast, but their short legs are meant for quick sprints to waiting cover and safety from predators — it is rare to catch one far from cover. Rockpiles, sage brush, old buildings and disgarded farm equipment are likely places to find cottontail.

I have found cottontail all over eastern Oregon, from Biggs Junction to Juntura, but my favorite area is the high desert from Bend south to Christmas Valley. Dozens of isolated dirt roads meander through hundreds of square miles of volcanic rock formations and thick sagebrush. This is perfect country for these little bunnies that are a thrill to hunt and great food for the table.

A semi-automatic .22 rifle is great sport but can be a bit dangerous. When alarmed, cottontail will often sprint for the rocks and ricochets can easily happen. A shotgun is quite safe and very sporting as these bunnies dodge through brush and over rocks. No need for anything larger than 20 gauge and the 410 bore is absolutely the perfect cottontail gun. A dog is helpful; however, two people hunting 50 yards apart will generally kick out most of the rabbits between them.

In addition to being a difficult and sporting target, they are great to eat. If you hunt in the summer, bring a cooler and some water. Clean rabbits soon after they are shot. Rabbits often carry fleas, and they can carry deadly diseases. Consider wearing rubber gloves when you handle rabbits either to clean them or pick them up. Cleaning the rabbits and taking care of the meat may seem like a lot of trouble but a meal of rabbit stew or fried cottontail is definitely worth the trouble.

Kids, dogs and cottontail rabbits are a traditional hunting combination. Valuable hunting experience and fine tablefare are gained while hunting cottontail. Chad Ekelund nailed this bunny near Fort Rock.

A predator call will increase a hunters chances to take bobcat and coyote.

COYOTES

To most folks, coyotes are the dastardly villains of the wilds. They rob chicken pens, kill deer and antelope fawns, ravage pheasant nests and are in general terms, no good for anything.

I feel differently. Coyotes are nature's tool for controlling certain animal populations when levels become too high for the carrying capacity of the habitat. They allow many forms of animal life to survive by allowing only the strong and most fit to survive. A coyote is the ultimate survivor. We have been trying to eliminate him for years and yet he still hangs on and, in fact, flourishes today. The coyote is one of the most intelligent and wary predators of all time. For this reason, good coyote hunters are few and far between.

Coyotes inhabit the entire state from north to south and east to west. Western Oregon has its share of "desert dogs." However, the dense vegetation makes deliberate hunting almost useless. I've taken several coyotes while stand-hunting bear and blacktail but these were just incidental kills. In addition, predator calls are not very effective on the westside. I can't say why.

Eastside coyote hunting is fine sport indeed but you must know what you are doing. Bill Smith was the manager for Oregon Department of Fish and Wildlife's Summer Lake Wildlife Management Area and an excellent coyote hunter. His advice on coyote hunting is worth repeating. "Go

Coyote hunting is not only great sport, but the pelts are quite valuable when taken mid-winter. Dan Campbell with a nice coyote shot near Juntura in southeastern Oregon.

about anywhere that is fairly isolated and look for sign. When you find lots of tracks situate yourself where you have a good view of a large area and hide against a tree or rock. Use a predator call that sounds like a dying rabbit. Call for only a couple of minutes then wait and watch for 15 or 20 minutes. If no luck, try again, then move to another area."

Coyote hunting is good all over most of eastern Oregon if you first scout the area. Some of the areas where I've had good shooting are: Wasco/Condon area in the John Day Canyon, Spray/Service Creek area, Fort Rock/Christmas Valley area, and the Summer Lake area.

Coyote pelts are worth some money. They bring from $20.00 to $60.00 depending on condition and color. Eastside dogs have better color and fur so they usually bring a higher price. A large hole in a pelt will reduce value considerably. Many hunters use high velocity 22's with full metal jacket bullets. The .22/250 is an excellent choice for coyote hunting. Whatever you choose to shoot, coyote hunting is great sport and Oregon has plenty of them. The season is open year round.

One thing I really like about varmint hunting is that it is an outdoor activity the entire family can participate in. My wife, Shirley, and I load our family in the camper and spend several weekends each summer chasing varmints on the eastside. Once we arrive, everyone joins in, young and old alike, and all have a great time. It gives the entire family a chance to practice firearm safety, burn a lot of powder and get close to nature. Isn't that what hunting is all about?

Oregon archer, Curt Mendenhall, with a tough trophy to collect with bow and arrow. This tom was taken in the Melrose unit of southwestern Oregon. (Photo courtesy Tim O'Kelly)

Chapter 12

BOWHUNTING

As I hike and hunt throughout Oregon, I am constantly reminded of the state's first true bowhunting experts, our native Indians. Years ago, I was hunting bear near a Clatsop County swamp when I lost my footing and grabbed for the nearest stable handhold, an overturned alder root-wad. After gaining my balance, I glanced down near my hand and noticed a shiny object protruding from the dirt under the root. It was an agate arrowhead in perfect condition. A strange sensation passed over my entire body — I was hunting in the shadow of early man.

Several years later another such incident occurred which gave me reason to stop and reflect on early Oregon hunters. I was walking down a well-used elk trail and feeling rather depressed. I had missed a rather simple shot at a beautiful spike elk earlier that morning and couldn't get the incident off my mind. The trail meandered through a dense stand of old-growth Douglas fir and I was following a mud path cut through the spongy moss by hundreds of years of deer and elk travel. I had to bend low under a vine maple that crossed the trail when I noticed a point sticking out of the green moss. It was a magnificent white six inch spear point with razor-like sharpness. Again I was following the footprints of early man as he hunted big game along the very trail I was walking.

The most eerie such experience happened last fall as I hunted mule deer near John Day. I had hunted hard for several days with no luck and hunters were everywhere. I decided to go far back into a primitive area and hopefully away from the many hunters I was meeting. I was several miles into the brush when I started to encounter deer. The trouble was it was so dry they'd hear me coming and bound away. I was hunting along a creek in a steep canyon when I came to a huge rock that completely blocked the canyon and overlooked the creek which cut a path around

Tim O'Kelly with a good Rocky Mountain bull taken in the Snake River country. (Photo courtesy Tim O'Kelly)

the blockage. The only way over was a primitive trail that led to the top. I decided to sit and hunt on this point which gave a commanding view of both the trail and the creek below. Any deer traveling the creek corridor had to pass within easy range of this spot. The thought occurred to me that if I were an early man, this is the location I would choose for an ambush. Just then I looked down and found a two inch black obsidian arrowhead with a broken point. I was a space-aged hunter with the same thoughts of an early Oregon bowhunter hundreds if not thousands of years before my time.

Oregon is a bowhunter's dream come true. The hunter who prefers the bow and arrow instead of, or in addition to the rifle will find abundant game and seasons here in Oregon. The skill required for an archer to take a big game animal is high and the success rate relatively low. The Oregon Department of Fish and Wildlife has apparently recognized this and it is reflected in the liberal seasons and limited restrictions. Oregon bowhunters can hunt six species of big game in addition to a variety of small game such as rabbits, ground squirrels, and coyotes.

A dyed-in-the-wool bowhunter, I am not. I am, however, an ardent hunter and in the "old days" before we had to choose a rifle or bow to hunt big game, I did both. Bow and arrow was a way to extend the rifle season and give me a second chance to collect that deer or elk. I learned, as a byproduct of those early years with bow and arrow, to respect the game I hunted, observe their habits, and become a better hunter in general. The very nature of bowhunting brings one closer to the game he hunts and elevates the hunting ethic.

It could be argued that a skilled bowhunter is far superior to a hunter who chooses the rifle. An archer must revert to his primitive instincts to bring him close to his quarry. The shot must be placed with near perfection to allow a clean and swift kill through bleeding action — an arrow delivers little if any shock to the animal. I recall my earliest lesson on this subject at the age of 12.

I was hunting small game with my primitive recurve near Seaside on a bright and sunny morning. I'd just taken an unsuccessful shot at a brush rabbit and was resharpening my broadhead when I heard the shrill chatter of a pine squirrel not more than 75 yards away. The stalk began and within minutes I was at full draw. My old Herters cedar shaft was pointing at the orange-bellied squirrel not 30 feet away. I let fly and the arrow flew true. It hit the squirrel squarely behind the front leg. Astonished, I watched that squirrel drag my arrow to the top of the spruce before dying from blood loss and stick in the branches high above. I lost my only broadhead but learned a valuable lesson about an arrow's lack of shock and how far a well-hit animal can travel before it bleeds out.

With the proper equipment, a bowhunter can kill the largest game

This massive cow elk was taken by Cliff Hamilton. Lots of great meat and a wonderful hunting experience were Cliff's reward for patience and a clean release.

North America has to offer. Before the days of compound bows and space-age arrowheads, I used a recurve with a 50 pound pull. It was effective on small game and I'd even managed to take a couple of nice blacktail but always felt insecure about tackling large coastal elk with such a light outfit. After all, a mature Roosevelt bull can approach 1,000 pounds of bone and muscle.

I was attending college at Oregon State University when my first opportunity to hunt elk occurred. My brother, Stan, had been watching a large herd near Seaside and wanted me to come down for a hunt on opening weekend. The plan was simple. he and a friend would stalk the herd near a field at daybreak and try for a shot. When the herd spooked, I would be waiting in the timber a quarter mile away along their well-used escape trail. The plan seemed too easy, but I was willing to try.

I arrived early and found the trail Stan had described with no problem. A fresh root-wad about 10 feet off the ground and only 30 feet from the trail would be my blind for the next half day. I set my bow with arrow readied at arms length, made myself comfortable, and began to study my homework which I had packed in. Only an hour or so had passed when I looked up to check the trail and could hardly believe my eyes. Before me were two large cows feeding with heads down, totally unaware of my presence. I must have made a noise as I grabbed the bow and they bounded off to a range of about 30 yards. I drew full, aimed for the lungs of the nearest cow, and let fly. At the "twang" of my string, they galloped off and one stopped less than 100 yards away. The timber was quite dark and the arrow appeared to have fallen short. I made a hasty stalk toward the lone elk hoping to get another shot as she retreated. I crept within about 50 yards and was about to draw my bow when the elk simply fell over and died. My initial shot was a good lung hit and the Bear razorhead was protruding from the other side of the huge cow elk! I have never since doubted the penetration and killing power of the bow and arrow.

ELK

The 14,000 bow and arrow enthusiasts who hunt elk in Oregon have plenty of elk hunting opportunity on both the east and west side. They killed nearly 1,500 elk in 1986. According to the 1987 Oregon Department of Fish and Wildlife's hunting synopsis, elk hunters have nearly a month of hunting time from late August to late September in both eastern and western Oregon. In both cases, hunters have opportunity to take either-sex. In addition, 4,000 antlerless controlled elk hunt tags were available in the Wilson, Alsea, and Tioga units during November and December. Be sure to check the most recent synopsis for details.

Oregon has approximately 55,000 Rocky Mountain elk east of the Cascades and bowhunters take their fair share each year. Few, however, are large enough to score high in the record book. Only 16 of the top 250

Noted bowhunter and game caller Larry D. Jones of Springfield, Oregon, who has built an industry around elk calling is perhaps is Oregon's best-known archer. Jones took this fine bull elk in the 1987 season.

Janelle Rusell with her first elk. It is the Rocky Mountain variety and this 6x6 was killed near John Day in central Oregon.

Dale Baumgartner's world record Roosevelt's elk is probably the greatest trophy ever taken by an Oregon archer. It scored 352 1/8 Pope and Young and was taken in 1985 in Tillamook County.

heads listed in the Pope and Young Record Book came from Oregon. William Sanowski took the largest bow and arrow-killed Rocky Mountain elk in Oregon in 1976. The rack had six points on each side, scored 364 6/8, and ranks 34 in the book.

Western Oregon has an estimated population of 59,000 elk and bowhunters interested in record-book Roosevelt's elk should give Oregon high consideration. Pope and Young lists a total of 86 Roosevelt's elk and 38 came from Oregon. Oregon has seven of the top 10 listed. Clatsop tops the list of counties where trophy bulls were taken, with 10. The largest Roosevelt's elk taken in Oregon is the current world record shot by Dale Baumgartner in 1985 in Tillamook County. It scored 352 1/8 and had seven points on the right and eight on the left antler. This is, in my opinion, the greatest feat ever accomplished by an Oregon bowhunter. His account of the hunt comes from the Bowhunting Big Game Records of North America third edition and is as follows:

"The big bull was working a drainage only a couple of miles from my house. It was an area I knew well, and I'd seen the bull two times before the season opened. In an old homestead clearing in the drainage, I had previously built a treestand. The nearest logging road was about a mile away, and I had cleared a trail for access to the meadow. During the season, I made many trips into the canyon to see if the elk were using the clearing. There wasn't much sign until the day before the season was to close.

"When I arrived that day I knew the elk were close by, and I went directly to the treestand. Before long I could hear elk back in the timber working toward the meadow.

"Two cows, two spikes, and a forked-horn entered the meadow cautiously. Just then the big bull bugled from somewhere behind them. Minutes later, he came trotting out into the meadow herding six more cows. He went directly after the lesser bulls and drove them out of the clearing. On his way back toward the cows, which were directly below my treestand by then, he stopped and tore heck out of a 10 foot fir tree.

"My arrow hit him hard in the chest as he walked directly past my stand. The bull bolted, about 10 yards before a second arrow hit him in the hindquarters. I hadn't lead him enough.

"From the stand I could see the bull standing in the timber for a few minutes. After waiting for what seemed a long time, I got out of the tree and went over to where I'd last seen the bull. Finding a big pool of blood and a good blood trail, I started after him. Using my flashlight, I followed the trail down toward the bottom of the canyon. It seemed as though he was just staying ahead of me. I could hear him but it was too dark to see him. Finally, I decided to head home and get help.

"Picking up the blood trail at first light the next day, I recovered the bull further down the canyon. With the help of two friends, it still took a day and a half to get him out."

DEER

Approximately 15,000 Oregonians enjoyed bowhunting for deer in 1986. They harvested nearly 3,500 animals and had a 22% success rate. Bowhunters have ample time and opportunity to pursue deer on both sides of the Cascade Mountains. Most of the state is open to bowhunting, restrictions are quite limited, and in most areas, hunters can take either-sex. In general, archers have a month to hunt deer from late August to late September. In addition, several units in northeast Oregon offered nearly 1,700 buck permits during 1987. Again, hunters should read the

Oregon archer Jeff Eggleston with the state record nontypical mule deer. It was taken in Lake County in 1986. It scored 224 and ranks 10th in the Pope and Young record book.

most recent hunting synopsis for current information.

Oregon definitely has its share of trophy blacktail. Almost 50% of blacktail listed in the 1987 Pope and Young Record Book were taken in Oregon,including the top four heads. The current world record and also Number Three was taken by B.G. Shurtleff in Marion County. The record head has seven points on each side and scores 172 2/8 points.

Both typical and nontypical mule deer are listed in Pope and Young. However, few came from Oregon. Of the top 250 typical and nontypical heads listed, only 5% came from Oregon. Oregon's best typical head was shot by Ronald Halpin in 1966 at Hart Mountain. It scored 178 points and was five points on each side. The largest nontypical mule deer was taken by Jeff Eggleston in 1986. It scored 224 points, ranks 10 and was killed in Lake County.

ANTELOPE

Controlled bowhunts for antelope have been offered by the Oregon Department of Fish and Wildlife in the Gerber Reservoir area in southcentral Oregon and in the Grizzly Unit of southeastern Oregon. About 500 tags are issued and the hunts take place in August and September. Chances for drawing a tag range from 50 to 100%.

Oregon bowhunters have placed only two pronghorns in Pope and

Tim O'Kelly with a cougar shot in the Dixon unit of southwestern Oregon. (Photo courtesy Tim O'Kelly.)

The largest California bighorn sheep ever killed in Oregon by bow and arrow was shot by Don Rajnus at Hart Mountain in southeastern Oregon. It scored 149 3/8 and was taken in 1982.

Young out of the top 125 listed. The largest ranks 33 and was killed by Harold Benson. It was shot near Gerber Reservoir in 1977 and scored 78 4/8. The right horn measured 16 4/8 inches and the left an even 16 inches.

BLACK BEAR

Bear may be hunted with bow and arrow concurrent with the rifle season.

Only two of the top 200 black bear ranked in Pope and Young have come from Oregon. The largest bear ever taken with bow and arrow in the Beaver State was shot by David Greisen in Jackson County in 1985. It ranks 119 and scored 20 5/16.

COUGAR

Cougar may be taken with bow and arrow and approximately 450 tags were available during the 1987 hunting season. Chance of drawing a tag ranges from 18 to 100% depending on the hunt you apply for. Seasons range from Nov. 15 through January. Cougar hunters must have access to well-trained dogs if they expect a reasonable chance for success. Few Oregon cougar have been ranked in the Pope and Young Record Book.

The largest cougar killed with a bow and arrow in Oregon was taken by Terrell Buchanan in 1973. It ranks 29, was killed in Wallowa County of northeastern Oregon, and scored 15 2/16.

BIGHORN SHEEP

Less than 50 bighorn sheep tags are offered each year in Oregon and bow and arrows are legal weapons. The largest and only head entered in Pope and Young was taken by Don Rajnus in Lake County in 1982. It scored 149 3/8 and ranks Number 68.

LEGAL WEAPONS

A 40 pound or greater longbow, recurve or compound bow can be used to hunt deer, black bear, antelope and cougar. A longbow, recurve or compound bow with a minimum pull of 50 pounds is required for elk and bighorn sheep. Broadheads must be at least 7/8 inch wide to hunt any big game animal in Oregon.

1986 ELK BOW SEASON

Units by Area	Hunters	HARVEST			Percent Hunter Success	Hunter Days
		Antlerless	Bulls	Total		
Saddle Mountain	1,166	56	37	93	8	11,640
Scappoose	167	0	0	0	0	1,749
Wilson	1,284	55	9	64	5	12,281
Trask	637	19	20	39	6	4,822
Stott Mountain	137	0	10	10	7	1,458
Alsea	519	32	11	43	8	4,426
Siuslaw	157	9	0	0	6	1,982
Willamette	88	0	0	0	0	538
NORTH COAST AREA	4,155	171	87	258	6	38,896
Applegate	10	0	0	0	0	60
Tioga	667	39	68	107	16	5,297
Sixes	29	0	0	0	0	203
Powers	118	0	0	0	0	836
Chetco	29	0	0	0	0	464
Evans Creek	20	0	0	0	0	160
Melrose	39	0	0	0	0	449
SOUTHWEST AREA	912	39	68	107	12	7,469
Santiam	559	0	11	11	2	5,257
Metolius	10	10	0	10	100	250
McKenzie	196	10	19	29	15	1,656
Upper Deschutes	255	0	0	0	0	2,472
Indigo	118	9	0	9	8	1,318
Fort Rock	157	0	9	9	6	1,236
Dixon	147	0	0	0	0	1,744
Rogue	441	0	0	0	0	4,420
Keno	49	10	0	10	20	451
CASCADE AREA	1,932	39	39	78	4	18,804
ROOSEVELT ELK TOTALS	6,999	249	194	443	6	65,169
Minam	186	0	20	20	11	1,880
Imnaha	137	10	10	20	15	1,341
Catherine Creek	127	19	10	29	23	1,563
Keating	39	0	0	0	0	302
Pine Creek	39	0	0	0	0	390
Lookout Mountain	59	0	0	0	0	443
WALLOWA ZONE	587	29	40	69	12	5,919
Snake River	98	0	29	29	30	1,107
Sled Springs	284	19	29	48	17	2,811
Wenaha	421	68	88	156	37	4,445
Walla Walla	304	30	40	70	23	2,206

Mt. Emily	431	28	18	46	11	5,005
WENAHA-SNAKE ZONE	1,538	145	204	344	23	15,574
Columbia Basin	108	0	20	20	14	893
Starkey	568	10	41	51	9	6,248
Ukiah	441	49	30	79	18	3,930
Sumpter	206	11	11	22	11	1,520
Desolation	372	21	20	41	11	3,661
Heppner	647	58	0	58	9	5,882
Fossil	108	0	0	0	0	1,149
UMATILLA-WHITMAN ZONE	2,450	149	122	271	11	23,283
Northside	294	10	20	30	10	2,146
Murderers Creek	274	20	60	80	29	2,417
Beulah	167	10	20	30	18	1,218
Malheur River	108	0	10	10	9	1,031
Silvies	304	19	38	57	19	2,736
Ochoco	784	12	12	24	3	8,497
Grizzly	167	0	0	0	0	1,827
Maury	39	0	0	0	0	312
OCHOCO-MALHEUR ZONE	2,137	71	160	231	11	20,184
BLUE MT. AREA TOTALS	6,712	394	526	920	14	64,960
Hood	108	10	0	10	9	1,011
White River	206	0	22	22	11	1,982
Silver Lake	10	0	10	10	100	100
Klamath Falls	20	0	0	0	0	140
Interstate	10	0	0	0	0	70
Steens Mtn.	0	0	0	0	0	0
Warner	0	0	0	0	0	0
Sprague	0	0	0	0	0	0
Biggs	10	0	0	0	0	70
Maupin	0	0	0	0	0	0
Paulina	31	0	10	10	32	103
CENTRAL AREA TOTALS	395	10	42	52	13	3,476
ROCKY MTN. ELK TOTALS	7,107	404	568	972	14	68,436
BOW SEASON TOTALS	14,106	653	762	1,415	10	133,605

Courtesy Oregon Department of Fish & Game

1986 DEER BOW SEASON

(Does not include the late controlled bow hunts)

Units by Area	Hunters	HARVEST Antlerless	HARVEST Buck	HARVEST Total	Percent Hunter Success	Hunter Days
Saddle Mountain	707	88	31	119	17	8,140
Scappoose	246	26	6	32	13	2,214
Wilson	921	41	14	55	6	7,731
Trask	584	47	46	93	16	5,230
Stott Mountain	130	7	13	20	15	1,469
Alsea	934	110	76	186	20	10,300
Siuslaw	195	0	34	34	17	1,976
Willamette	662	73	60	133	20	6,841
NORTH COAST AREA	**4,379**	**392**	**280**	**672**	**15**	**43,901**
Tioga	474	71	90	161	34	5,188
Sixes	58	7	20	27	47	412
Powers	45	13	6	19	42	238
Chetco	78	7	7	14	18	949
Applegate	188	13	45	58	31	1,666
Evans Creek	214	13	83	96	45	3,035
Melrose	143	20	14	34	24	1,612
SOUTHWEST AREA	**1,200**	**144**	**265**	**409**	**34**	**13,100**
Santiam	1,200	72	132	204	17	11,286
McKenzie	499	77	84	161	32	5,165
Indigo	136	13	58	71	52	1,379
Dixon	234	26	7	33	14	2,476
Rogue	1,148	90	186	276	24	11,214
CASCADE AREA	**3,217**	**278**	**467**	**745**	**23**	**21,362**
WESTERN OREGON TOTAL	**8,796**	**814**	**1,012**	**1,826**	**21**	**78,363**
Minam	91	7	14	21	23	715
Imnaha	58	7	14	21	36	541
Catherine Creek				– NO SEASON –		
Keating				– NO SEASON –		
Pine Creek				– NO SEASON –		
Lookout Mountain				– NO SEASON –		
WALLLOWA ZONE	**149**	**14**	**28**	**42**	**28**	**1,256**
Snake River	58	0	14	14	24	644
Chesnimnus				– NO SEASON–		
Sled Springs	221	13	78	91	41	1,885
Wenaha	97	0	19	19	20	989
Walla Walla	162	13	32	45	28	1,445
Mt. Emily	221	6	56	62	28	2,372
WENAHA-SNAKE ZONE	**759**	**32**	**199**	**231**	**30**	**7,335**

Starkey	441	26	98	124	28	3,638
Ukiah			– NO SEASON –			
Sumpter	272	0	57	57	21	2,811
Desolation	577	0	31	31	5	6,243
Heppner	182	6	44	50	27	1,593
Fossil	58	0	0	0	0	451
Columbia Basin			– NO SEASON –			
UMATILLA-WHITMAN ZONE	**1,530**	**32**	**230**	**262**	**17**	**14,736**
Northside	169	0	37	37	22	1,326
Murderers Creek	188	0	45	45	24	1,593
Beulah	188	0	102	102	54	1,322
Malheur River	78	0	13	13	17	851
Silvies	72	0	106	106	41	3,296
Ochoco	928	26	155	181	20	7,489
Grizzly	195	6	25	31	16	1,794
Maury	52	0	14	14	27	540
OCHOCO-MALHEUR ZONE	**1,870**	**32**	**497**	**529**	**28**	**18,211**
BLUE MTN. AREA TOTAL	**4,308**	**110**	**954**	**1,064**	**25**	**41,538**
Biggs	39	0	0	0	0	533
Maupin	45	0	0	0	0	186
Hood	156	0	28	28	18	1,268
White River	130	0	14	14	11	1,190
Metolius	149	6	6	12	8	1,257
Paulina	117	0	21	21	18	1,267
Upper Deschutes	461	20	77	77	17	4,039
Fort Rock	344	6	66	86	25	3,375
Silver Lake	162	0	12	18	11	1,069
Sprague	13	0	7	7	54	72
Klamath Falls	143	0	72	72	50	1,183
Keno	169	0	61	61	36	1,813
Interstate	52	0	14	14	27	748
Warner	156	0	79	79	51	1,560
CENTRAL AREA	**2,136**	**32**	**457**	**489**	**23**	**19,560**
Wagontire	0	0	0	0	0	0
Beatys Butte	32	0	6	6	19	211
Juniper	19	0	0	0	0	76
Steens Mountain	6	0	6	6	100	60
Whitehorse	19	0	6	6	32	114
Owyhee	53	7	27	34	65	358
HI-DESERT AREA	**129**	**7**	**45**	**52**	**40**	**819**
EASTERN OREGON TOTAL	**6,573**	**149**	**1,456**	**1,605**	**24**	**61,917**
STATE TOTAL	**15,369**	**963**	**2,468**	**3,431**	**22**	**140,280**

Courtesy Oregon Department of Fish & Game

One of the real challenges of hunting mule deer in Oregon is to seek them in open country such as shown in this photograph.

Appendix A

1988 LICENSE AND TAG FEES
License and Tag Fees are not refundable.

RESIDENT
Resident Hunter's License, $9.50
Resident Combination Angler's and Hunter's License, $19.50
Resident Antelope Tag (1,2), $25.50
Resident Bear Tag (1), $10.50
Resident Bighorn Sheep Tag (1,2), $90.50
Resident Cougar Tag (1,2), $50.50
Resident Deer Tag (1), $7.50
Resident Elk Tag (1), $19.50
Controlled Hunt Application Fee, $3.00
*Disabled War Veteran License (residents only), free
*Pioneer Hunting License (65 years old-50 years immediate prior residence in state), $1.50
Pioneer and Disabled Vet Elk Tag (1), $3.00
*Senior Citizens Hunting and Fishing License (70 years old-5 years immediate residence in state), free

NONRESIDENT
Nonresident Hunter's License, $100.50
Nonresident Antelope Tag (1,2), $125.50
Nonresident Bear Tag (1), $75.50
Nonresident Bighorn Sheep Tag (1,2), $900.50
Nonresident Cougar Tag (1,2), $150.50
Nonresident Deer Tag (1), $75.50
Nonresident Elk Tag (1), $165.50
Controlled Hunt Application Fee, $3.00

1. Hunter's License also required.
2. Available by application only.
* These licenses may be obtained by mail or in person through the Portland Office. Applications are available at Regional Offices.

GENERAL REGULATIONS

Shooting Hours — Game mammals may only be hunted from one-half hour before sunrise to one-half hour after sunset.

Vehicles, Boats, Aircraft — No person shall:
1. Hunt any wildlife from a motor-propelled vehicle.
2. Communicate information on the location of game mammals from an aircraft.
3. Hunt within six hours after having been transported by helicopter to any point other than an established airport adequate for fixed-wing aircraft.
4. Shoot at antelope from a point within 50 yards of a motor-propelled vehicle including aircraft.

Prohibited Areas — No person shall:
1. Shoot from or across a public road.
2. Hunt on any refuge closed by the state or federal government.
3. Hunt within the corporate limits of any city or town, public park or cemetery, or on any campus or grounds of a public school, college, university or from a public road or road right-of-way.
4. Hunt game mammals outside any area designated by a controlled hunt tag when such tag is required for that hunt season.

Prohibited Methods — No person shall:
1. Hunt for or kill any wildlife for another person.
2. Hunt any game mammal with dogs, EXCEPT bear, cougar and silver gray squirrel.
3. Use an artificial light for hunting game mammals.
4. Cast from or within 500 feet of a motor vehicle an artificial light upon any game mammals, predatory animals or livestock while having in possession or immediate physical presence a weapon with which the game mammals or livestock could be killed.
5. Take game mammals with trap or snare.
6. Use any drug or chemical to hunt or kill any game mammal.
7. Hunt during a controlled elk hunt with a centerfire or muzzleloading rifle unless the appropriate unused controlled hunt elk tag or unused cougar tag valid for the time period and area being hunted is in possession.

Disguising Sex, Waste and Sale — No person shall:
1. Disguise the sex or kind of any wildlife while in the field or in transit from the field.
2. Waste game mammals or parts thereof, except that the meat of cougar need not be salvaged.
3. Sell or offer for sale, barter or exchange, any game mammals or parts thereof EXCEPT deer, elk and antelope hides and deer and elk antlers used for handcrafted items.
4. Possess the meat or carcass of any deer or elk without the animal's scalp while in the field or in transit from the field. The scalp shall include the attached eyes and ears, if female; or the ears, antlers and eyes if the animal is a male.

Trespass — No person shall:
1. Hunt on the cultivated or enclosed land of another without permission. Enclosed land may be bounded by a fence, ditch, water or any other line indicating separation from surrounding territory.

Other Restrictions — No person shall:
1. Take or hold in captivity the young of any game mammal.
2. Hold in captivity any wildlife of this state for which a permit is required without first securing a permit.

3. Release without a permit any wildlife brought from another state or country, or raised in captivity in this state.

4. Resist game enforcement officers.

5. Hunt protected wildlife.

6. Hunt in Safety Zones created and posted by the Department of Fish and Wildlife.

7. Operate or be transported in a motor-propelled vehicle in violation of Cooperative Travel Management Area restrictions. Cooperative Travel Management Areas are listed in the Deer, Elk and Silver Gray Squirrel Regulations.

8. Disturb, damage, remove, alter or possess any official Department signs.

TAGGING, POSSESSION, AND TRANSPORTATION

When the owner of a game mammal tag kills a game mammal for which a tag is issued, he shall immediately remove in its entirety only the month and day of the kill and attach the tag in plain sight securely to the game mammal. The tag shall be kept attached to such carcass or parts thereof so long as the same are preserved. No person shall possess the meat or carcass of any deer or elk without the animal's scalp while in the field or in transit from the field. The scalp shall include the attached eyes and ears, if female; or ears, antlers and eyes if the animal is male.

No person shall have in possession any game mammal tag from which all or part of any date has been removed or mutilated except when the tag is legally validated and attached to a game mammal.

When the game mammal or part thereof is transferred to the possession of another person, a written record describing the game mammal or part being transferred and the name and address of the person whose tag was originally attached to the carcass, and the number of that tag, shall accompany such transfer and shall remain with such game mammal or part so long as the same is preserved.

All game mammals in possession in the field or forest, or in transit more than 48 hours after the close of the open season for such mammal, must be tagged by the Department of Fish and Wildlife or Oregon State Police.

All game mammals or portions thereof shipped by commercial carrier must be tagged by the Department of Fish and Wildlife or Oregon State Police.

No person shall receive or have in possession any game mammal or part thereof which: (1) is not properly tagged; (2) was taken in violation of any wildlife laws or regulations; or (3) was taken by any person who is or may be exempt from the jurisdiction of such laws or regulations.

No person shall possess or transport any game mammal or part thereof which has been illegally killed, found or killed for humane reasons unless they have notified and received permission from personnel of the Oregon State Police or Department of Fish and Wildlife prior to transporting.

ARMS AND AMMUNITION

Hunting for game mammals with any weapon other than those authorized by season is prohibited. The breakdown is as follows: for hunting seasons designated as rifle hunts, hunters may use any firearm legal for that species; for hunting seasons designated as muzzleloading hunts, hunters may only use the muzzleloading rifles legal for that species; for hunting seasons designated for bowhunting, hunters may only use the bows legal for that species — no firearms may be on your person while bowhunting; for controlled antlerless deer seasons, hunters may use any weapon legal for deer.

.22 Centerfire Rifle or .22 Centerfire Handgun: deer, bear, antelope, cougar. Hunters

Shirley Johnson took this rockchuck near Redmond, Oregon, using a .222 Remington.

wishing to hunt deer with a handgun must have their deer tag validated for "Handgun Hunting Only" before the hunt's opening date. Validation stamps are available at all Portland, Regional and District Offices of the Department. No rifles may be in possession while hunting. Fully automatic rifles prohibited. Semiautomatic rifles with a magazine capacity of more than five cartridges are prohibited.

.24 centerfire Rifle: elk and bighorn sheep.

Shotgun using slugs or #1 or larger buckshot: deer, bear, antelope and cougar.

.40 Muzzleloader: deer, bear, antelope and cougar. Only iron sights and open ignition allowed.

.50 Muzzleloader: elk and bighorn sheep. Only iron sights and open ignition allowed.

40 lb. Longbows, Recurve and Compound Bows: deer, bear, antelope and cougar. Broadheads must be at least 7/8" wide.

50 lb. Longbows, Recurve and Compound Bows: elk and bighorn sheep. Broadheads must be at least 7/8" wide.

Any Rifle, Handgun, Shotgun, Muzzleloader, Longbow, Recurve Bow or Compound Bow: silver gray squirrels.

Appendix B

OREGON DEPARTMENT OF FISH AND WILDLIFE REGIONAL OFFICES

Director — Randy Fisher
Portland Office — 506 SW Mill St., P.O. Box 59, 97207
   (229-5403)
Northwest — Rt. 5, Box 325, Corvallis 97330, (757-4186)
Southwest — 4192 N Umpqua Hwy, Roseburg 97470, (440-3353)
Central — 61374 Parrell Road, Bend 97702, (388-6363)
Northeast — 107 20th St., La Grande 97850, (963-2138)
Southeast — Box 8, Hines 97738, (573-6582)
Marine — Marine Science Dr., Bldg. 3, Newport 97365
   (867-4741)
Columbia — 17330 SE Evelyn St., Clackamas 97015, (657-2000)

OREGON STATE POLICE

State Office — 107 Public Service Bldg., Salem 97310

NATIONAL FOREST SUPERVISORS' OFFICES

Deschutes — 1645 Hwy 20 E., Bend 97701 (382-6922)

Fremont — 34 N. G St., Box 551, Lakeview, OR 97630 (947-2151)

Malheur — 139 N.E. Dayton St., John Day, OR 97845 (575-1731)

Mt. Hood — 2955 N.W. Division, Gresham, OR 97030 (666-0700)

Ochoco — 155 N. Court, Box 490, Prineville, OR 97754 (447-6247)

Rouge River — Federal Bldg., 333 W. 8th St., Box 520,
   Medford, OR, 97501 (776-3600)

Sisklyou — 200 N.E. Greenfield Rd., Box 440, Grants Pass, OR
   97526 (479-5301)

Sluslaw — 4077 Research Way, Box 1148, Corvallis, OR 97333
   (479-5301)

Umatilla — 2517 S.W. Hailey Ave., Pendleton, OR 97801
(276-3811)

Umpqua — 2900 N.W. Stewart Pkwy., Box 1008, Roseburg, OR 97470
(672-6601)

Wallowa-Whitman — 1550 Dewey Ave., Box 907, Baker, OR 97814
(523-6391)

Willamette — Federal Bldg., 211 E. 7th Ave., Box 10607,
Eugene, OR 97440 (687-6522)

Winema — Post Office Bldg., 2nd Floor, 7th & Walnut St.,
Box 1390, Klamath Falls, OR 97601 (883-6714)

UNITED STATES DEPARTMENT OF THE INTERIOR
BUREAU OF LAND MANAGEMENT

Oregon State Office — 825 N.E. Multnomah St., Box 2965,
Portland, OR 97208 (231-6251)

Lakeview District — 1000 Ninth St. S., Box 151, Lakeview, OR
97630 (947-2177)

Klamath Falls Resource Area — 1939 S. 6th, Box 369, Klamath
Falls, OR 97601 (883-6916)

Burns District — 74 S. Alvord St., Burns, OR 97720 (573-5241)

Prineville District — 185 E. 4th St., Box 550, Prineville, OR
97754 (447-4155)

Salem District — 1717 Fabry Rd. S.E., Salem, OR 97302
(399-5646)

Tillamook Resource Area — 6615 Officer's Row, Tillamook, OR
97141 (842-7546)

Eugene District — 1255 Pearl St., Box 10226, Eugene, OR 97401
(687-6650)

Roseburg District — 777 N.W. Garden Valley Blvd., Roseburg, OR
97470 (672-4491)

Medford District — 3040 Biddle Rd., Medford, OR 97501
(776-4174)

Coos Bay District — 333 S. 4th St., Coos Bay, OR 97420
(269-5880)

Vale District — 100 Oregon St., Box 700, Vale, OR 97918
(473-3144)

Baker Resource Area — Box 987, Baker, OR 97814 (523-6391)

Some muzzleloader hunts are offered for mule deer in Oregon.